THE
Queen's
Pirate

SIR FRANCIS DRAKE &
THE GOLDEN HIND

THE
Queen's
Pirate

SIR FRANCIS DRAKE &
THE GOLDEN HIND

KEVIN JACKSON

London and New York

The Queen's Pirate
Sir Francis Drake & The Golden Hind
9 8 7 6 5 4 3 2 1

First published by TSB, 2020

Published in 2021 in the United States by
Leapfrog Press Inc.
P.O. Box 1293
Dunkirk, New York 14048

Distributed in the United States by
Consortium Book Sales and Distribution
St. Paul, Minnesota 55114
www.cbsd.com

Cover, text and map design: James Shannon
Set in Adobe Garamond Pro and 1689 GLC Garamond Pro

ISBN: 978-1-948585-18-7 (paperback)

Printed and bound in the United Kingdom by TJ Books Ltd

About the Author – Kevin Jackson

Kevin Jackson was an English writer, broadcaster and film-maker. He had also been a Teaching Fellow of Vanderbilt University, Nashville; a radio producer and television director for the BBC; Associate Arts Editor for *The Independent* and a roving reporter for *Night and Day* Magazine, where his assignments included a week on a fishing boat in Atlantic waters, a training mission on a Royal Navy aircraft carrier and a helicopter flight to an oil rig in the Caspian, near Baku. His books include *Constellation of Genius* (Hutchinson), a history of modernism which was a Book of the Week in *The Guardian* and a Book of the Year in the *Express*; *Invisible Forms* (Picador); *Carnal* (Pallas Athene); and the authorized biography *Humphrey Jennings* (Picador). He collaborated with the cartoonist Hunt Emerson on several projects, including *Bloke's Progress* (Ruskin Comics), a comic fable inspired by the writings of John Ruskin; a version of Dante's *Inferno* (Knockabout); and, most recently, *Lives of the Great Occultists* (Knockabout). His long narrative poem, *Greta and the Labrador* (Holland House Books) was charmingly illustrated by the artist Jo Dalton. Jackson's other regular collaborators included the cameraman Spike Geilinger, who shot most of his independent films, and the musician Colin Minchin, with whom he co-wrote the rock opera *Bite*. He was a Fellow of the Royal Society of Arts, a Companion of the Guild of St George, and a Regent of the Collège de 'Pataphysique. At his untimely death, Kevin Jackson had completed four of the titles in his Seven Ships Maritime History series. We hope to publish Captain Cook's *Endeavour* in due course. Though each volume tells an independent tale, the series also charts the rise and decline of Britain as the world's greatest naval power.

TSB | Can of Worms will proudly publish Kevin Jackson's wonderful homage to TE Lawrence: *Legion: Thirteen Ways of Looking at Lawrence of Arabia* in 2022. Many moving obituaries were published shortly after Kevin Jackson's death, and links can be found at: www.canofworms.net/KevinJackson.

Production and Publishing Credits

A considerable number of people are involved in realizing an author's work as a finished book on the shelf of your local library, bookshop or online retailer. TSB would like to acknowledge the critical input of:

Cover design, layout and cartography. TSB/Can of Worms has benefited from a longstanding relationship with James Shannon on book production and website development for many of its own titles as well as some of Can of Worms's consultancy clients. For this *Seven Ships Maritime History* Series, James has undertaken the cover design, page layout as well as map design. James and further examples of his work can be found at: www.jshannon.com

Editorial. Editorial has been provided by Tobias Steed, publisher of TSB/Can of Worms. Tobias's career in publishing has spanned forty plus years having started as an editorial assistant for Johns Hopkins University Press in Baltimore, co-founder of illustrated travel guides publishing company, Compass American Guides, Oakland, California, Associate Publisher and Director of New Media at Fodor's/Random House, New York, and most recently founder and publisher of Can of Worms Enterprises Ltd. www.canofworms.net

Ship Plans. Permission for the use of the ship plans in the *Seven Ships Maritime History* series* have been provided to TSB/Can of Worms by Vadiim Eidlin at Best Ship Models, a company that provides accurate ship plans designed especially for model shipbuilders. Their collection includes 500+ plans for beginners and professional modelers. www.bestshipmodels.com

*the plans used in *Darwin's Odyssey: The Voyage of the Beagle* are from Alamy.com

Sales and Marketing. Sales and Marketing. Sales and Marketing for the Seven Ships Maritime History and all other Leapfrog Press titles is overseen by Consortium Book Sales and Distribution (CBSD) St. Paul, Minnesota 55114 www.cbsd.com

Publicity. All publicity enquiries should be directed to Mary Bisbee-Beek. leapfrog@leapfrogpress.com. Further information and resources for the Seven Ships Maritime History series can be found at www.leapfrogpress.com

Seven Ships Maritime History Series – a Note from the author

In the summer of 2006, about five years before the Syrian Civil War began, I spent a couple of weeks in Damascus. In theory I was doing some informal research about Lawrence of Arabia, but in reality I mostly wandered the streets and gazed at the buildings and was touched by the exquisite good manners of the local people. In the afternoons, when the heat became oppressive for a pale European, I went into the Umayyad Mosque – infidels are quite welcome there – and squatted next to one of the pillars, and read the book I had brought with me: a hardback edition of Livingstone Lowes' *The Road to Xanadu,* which is a wonderful exploration of all the travel narratives that fed the imagination of the young Coleridge. It was delicious to escape from the uncomfortable warmth of a Damascene summer and daydream about the snow and the icebergs and the dark, chill waters that the ancient mariners had met when they ventured to the far north.

The extracts from old diaries and letters and memoirs cited in this study re-awoke in me that sense of wonder which the best sailors' tales have always inspired, especially in children. When I put the book down to daydream, I began to think of how fascinating it would be for me to find out more about maritime history, and to tell the stories of the greatest British ships over the centuries of the Western maritime expansion. It was not hard to choose seven famous vessels for seven books, each of which would have its own major themes: *Golden Hind* (exploration, plunder), *Mayflower* (religion, emigration), *Endeavour* (science, colonialism), *Bounty* (rebellion, survival), *Victory* (war, heroism), *Beagle* (biology, genius) and *Endurance* (leadership, heroism, survival). Each volume would be self-contained, but would also mark a chapter in the rise and decline of British maritime power and the creation of the modern world.

The idea came to me whole, in a single dreamy afternoon, and I knew it was what I wanted to do next. Now all I had to do was write my tales: the stories of Seven Ships.

Kevin Jackson, 2020

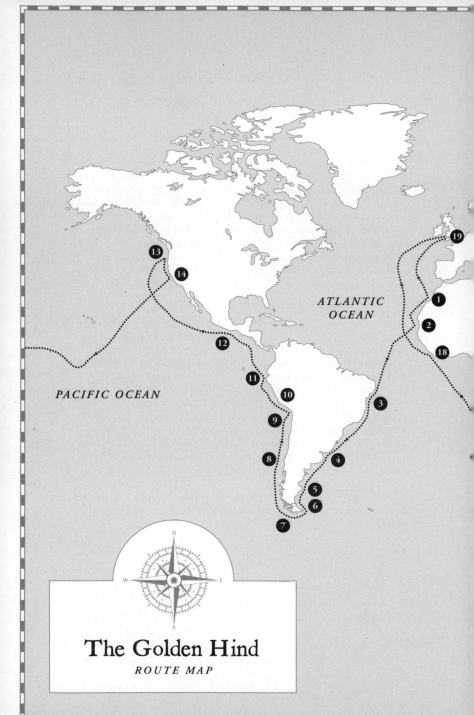

ATLANTIC
OCEAN

PACIFIC OCEAN

The Golden Hind
ROUTE MAP

PACIFIC OCEAN

1. Mogador December 1577
2. Cabo Blanco January 1578
3. Salvador
4. Rio de la Plata 5 April 1578
5. Bahia de los Nodales June 1578
6. Straits of Magellan 20 August 1578
7. Cape Horn 6 September 1578
8. Valparaiso 8 December 1578
9. Arica
10. Lima 15 February 1579

11. Guayaquill
12. Huatuico 15 April 1579
13. Oregon Dunes 5 June 1579
14. Cape Mendocino 17 June 1579
15. Palau October 1579
16. Timor November 1579
17. Cape of Good Hope
18. Sierra Leone 22 July 1580
19. Plymouth 26 September 1580

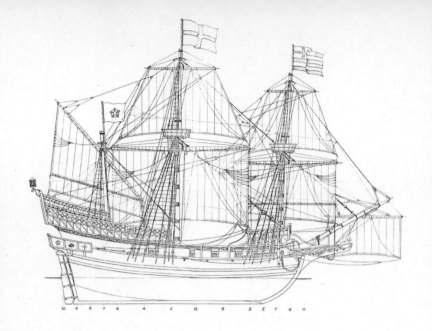

THE GOLDEN HIND

Launched: 1577
Tonnage: 100 – 150 tons
Displacement: 300 tons
Length: 102 feet (31m) on deck

Beam: 20 feet (6.1m)
Draught: 9 feet (2.7m)
Sail area: 386m²

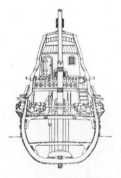

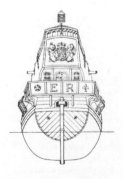

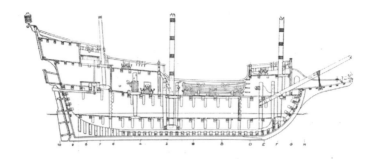

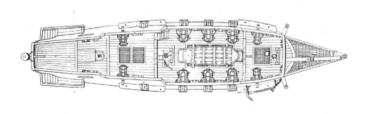

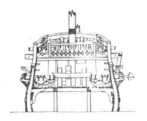
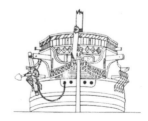

Table of Contents

Chapter One

A Tree in Darien

I t was mid-morning, 11 February 1573, the sun intensely bright and the day already growing uncomfortably warm and muggy. The English sea-captain and pirate Mr Francis Drake – he would not be *Sir* Francis until 1581 – was making his way westwards on foot through the pine forests of Panama, with plunder in mind. His plan was to make a surprise attack on one or more of the Spanish mule trains that were carrying immense amounts of gold and silver from mines in Peru, so that it could be put on board treasure ships and sent back to Spain, which was now the most powerful country in the Western world.

With him was a small company from his ship's crew. At the age of 33, Drake was almost two decades older than most of his shipmates – 18 young men and boys, most of them from his own county of Devon, in the south-west of England. They were, in effect, a band of guerrillas, passing stealthily through enemy territory, since Spanish forces had almost complete possession of the country.

The English force was attended by a band of friendly, reliable native guides, known as "Cimaroons", all ferociously hostile to the Spanish colonists in Panama and, thus, delighted to join Drake's expeditionary team. It had been six exhausting days since the team had set out from their ship's mooring on the Atlantic coastline, and the march had mostly been uphill, first through wet, steamy jungle, now through trees.

Spanish warships patrolled the Atlantic seaboard, behind them, and there was a large Spanish garrison ahead of them, in Panama City. They had to move quietly, sending a couple of Cimaroons ahead to scout. If they encountered anyone, the scouts would run back and the expedition would vanish into the depths of the forest before anyone could spot them and raise the alarm. The English boys carried nothing but their arms, since the Cimaroons had generously insisted on taking on the burden of all the other kit and provisions. The ship's crew were under strict orders not to kill women, children, or unarmed men, and also to enforce this rule on their guides, who would willingly have massacred Spaniards of any age or sex.

The march had fallen into a daily routine. It was much too hot to move in the middle hours of the day, so they walked in the early mornings and late evenings, making camp at night when it was refreshingly cool. Drake had used their midnight rests as a chance to teach the Cimaroons the Lord's Prayer in English, but without much success.

As they pushed upwards through the pines, the chief of their Cimaroon escort, a man they knew by the name the Spanish had given him, "Pedro", suddenly called a halt, and pointed forward. Peering through the dense covering trees, Drake could just make out that a short walk ahead of them was a slightly higher peak, marking the watershed of the Cordilleras. This was the landmark he had hoped to find.

Encouraged by this discovery, the company pushed on with renewed vigour, and soon had climbed the peak. Here, Pedro took Drake by the hand, and led him to a tall tree. Drake noticed that steps had been cut into its trunk, and that high up among the branches was a look-out platform, large enough for about a dozen men to stand on. Pedro climbed the steps, and Drake followed. He looked around.

Behind him to the east, he could see the Atlantic Ocean. To the west…well, he knew at once that it was the "Southern Ocean" or the "Secret Ocean", that much-discussed but largely unknown mass of water that Magellan had called "the Pacific". No Englishman had ever enjoyed this simultaneous vista of both oceans; nor had many Europeans. Among that select number, sixty years earlier, was Vasco Nunez de Balboa, the Spanish commander at the Darien Isthmus, who had climbed the very same tree in 1513. Two centuries or so later, the English Romantic poet John Keats evoked that vision in one of his most famous sonnets, "On First Looking Into Chapman's Homer" – though Keats made a famous blunder, wrongly identifying the bold explorer not as Balboa but as Cortez:

> *Then felt I like some watcher of the skies*
> *When a new planet sweeps into his ken;*
> *Or like stout Cortez when with eagle eyes*
> *He stared at the Pacific – and all his men*
> *Looked at each other with a wild surmise –*
> *Silent, upon a peak in Darien.*

The records tell us that Balboa, a good Catholic and patriotic Spaniard, had at once prayed to God and the Blessed Virgin Mary to "give him good success to subdue these lands to the glory of His name and the increase of the true religion." Accompanied by his men, he marched down to the waterfront, waded up to his waist into the sea, raised his sword and his shield and asked for the company to bear witness that he had taken possession of the ocean – "and all that appertains to it" – for the King of Castile and Leon.

Balboa's water-grab for Spain had remained unchallenged by any other nation, and Spanish rule of the Pacific was all but absolute. But Drake had other ideas. This sea, he fervently believed, ought to be the property of *his* country and his Queen, Elizabeth I. Like Balboa before him, Drake fell to his knees, thanked Almighty God for this miraculous vision, and prayed to Him to make it possible to sail across these new waters some day soon as captain of an English ship.

Then he summoned up the other English men and boys so that they could share this wonderful view, and he told them about his prayers for a great adventure into the Pacific. One of the company, John Oxenham, vowed that "unless our Captain did beat him from his company, he would follow him by God's grace."

From that point on, Drake was a man in the grip of an obsession. He vowed that one day he would sail into the Pacific, and wrest it from the hands of Spain.

Chapter Two

Enter the Dragon

The Spanish, who started to pay attention to the danger posed by this upstart English pirate some time in the early 1570s, knew him by several names: *Diaz*; *Draq*; *El Draque*. But in the long run he was most commonly known as *El Draco*: The Dragon. By the time Sir Francis Drake played his triumphant part in the defeat of the Spanish Armada in 1588 – one of the truly decisive significant sea battles in British history – they identified their deadly enemy as the Devil himself. Only diabolic agency, they believed, could account for his triumphs.

Born into obscure and humble circumstances, he had become one of the most famous men in the Western world. Drake's life ranks with that of Napoleon as one of the dozen or so most astonishing rags-to-riches stories of the last thousand years. And though he reached his prime in age of great English explorers and warriors – Sir Walter Raleigh, Sir Martin Frobisher, Sir Philip Sidney – Drake was the brightest star in that Elizabethan firmament.

Nobody else came close.

His countrymen adored him, not simply because he captured or sank so many enemy ships, nor because he brought home vast quantities of gold and silver, but for the sheer dash and audacity with which he carried out his raids. They saw in him their own image – or an image of what they might be, at their best. His enemies came to dread him. Spanish sailors were terrified whenever they heard that Drake was sailing against them; while Spanish mothers at home would frighten their children into obedience by telling them that the English Devil would come and eat them.

The myth of Drake, already potent in his own lifetime, grew and grew from the early seventeenth century onwards, when propagandists for the rise of British sea power set him up as the chief exemplar of daring, enterprise, patriotism, Protestantism and military genius. The process began in his lifetime, and gathered momentum in 1628, with the publication of *The World Encompassed by Sir Francis Drake* – a narrative of the circumnavigation compiled from notes made by Francis Fletcher, who was chaplain on the expedition. It urged young Englishmen to give up their foppish and effete ways, and to model themselves on their nation's hero.

Not until the time of Nelson, more than two centuries later, was there a sailor to rival him in his country's admiration. Many of the things that were said of him were in large part fanciful, such as the charming but almost certainly false yarn that he carried on nonchalantly playing a game of bowls when he first had word of the Armada sailing up the English Channel. It hardly matters: the story struck a deep chord in the English imagination. One of the country's most enduring legends is that Arthur and his knights are sleeping in a cave somewhere, ready to wake up and do battle when Britain is in peril; a national myth of the Victorian era reassured his countrymen that Drake's drum will pound out a loud warning when the enemy is approaching.

The patriotic myth of Drake reached its peak in the nineteenth century, when Britain possessed the global empire that Queen Elizabeth's magician, Dr John Dee, had both predicted and planned. But the legend survived, in milder forms, well into the twentieth and twenty-first centuries. Until recently, one of the standard British coins carried an image of the *Golden Hind*, the small ship in which Drake circumnavigated the world from 1577-1580.

Not until the last few decades, when indignation at all forms of colonialism has grown fierce and widespread, did anyone suggest that his violent aggressions were anything other than bold and thrilling adventures. Today's students of history are more likely to see him as a gangster and a thug: highly successful at his own types of crime.

And yet no amount of historical revisionism can make him seem insignificant. By any reckoning, Drake was a remarkable man, and an exceptionally brave one; possibly the greatest navigator of his age; a military strategist of impulsive, untutored genius; and a visionary, venturesome soul. This was the age when England had declined from its former power just a couple of centuries earlier into a somewhat poor and minor kingdom off the coast of continental Europe. In the Western world, the big powers were France, Portugal and, above all, Spain. Under Elizabeth, the English began to dream again of wealth and power. Drake was the man who might make those dreams come true.

Chapter Three

Character

What was he like? One of Drake's contemporaries, the historian John Stow, described him as "low of stature, of strong limb, broad-breasted, round-headed, brown hair, full-bearded, his eyes round, large and clear, well-favoured face, and of a cheerful countenance." Most other accounts tally with this, as do the several portraits made in the years after his triumphal return from his journey around the world in 1580. Though always vigorous and restless, Drake was fond of his food and wine, and in his later life began to grow stout. When not absorbed in his tasks, he was generally "merry", and enjoyed hearty good-humour and simple, sometimes childish, jokes.

He was, we can guess, not much given to introspection — at least, only one or two of the letters, diaries and speeches he wrote give evidence of what his inner life might have been. But many of his colleagues and his enemies recorded their own impressions, and, allowing for the excesses of hostility or adulation, a clear picture emerges.

The flaws in his nature are often closely bound up with his virtues. His courage could lead him into potentially disastrous recklessness. He was a brilliant improviser of naval strategy on the spur of the moment, but sometimes grew too impatient to make long-term plans; his forte was the surprise attack. He was passionate in his emotions – the English had not yet taken up the policy of the Stiff Upper Lip – and would often fly into rages that struck some as being like temper tantrums. He bore grudges, and craved revenge for even small slights.

Drake could be boastful (but he had good cause to brag). Throughout his life, he was deeply self-conscious about his low origins, and craved not only wealth but all the formal trappings of nobility – his knighthood and other titles, his coat of arms, his second marriage into an aristocratic family. He was, in short, something of a snob, a little too readily impressed by lords and fine gentlemen. But his craving for dignity was a matter of practicality as well as self-conceit: as late as the battle against the Armada, he was denied high command because of his low origins. The higher he climbed the social ladder, the more power he could wield.

On the other hand, he never lost his common touch, and when it was needed, would always throw himself into heavy manual labour at the side of his men. And if at times he yielded to dark suspicions, and thought that powerful men were plotting against him – well, the Elizabethan court really was a place of plots and counterplots, oaths and betrayals, and sometimes Drake had every cause for mild paranoia: people *were* plotting against him.

Perhaps the most surprising of his qualities to modern eyes is the intensity and consistency of his faith. He was a

Christian, in a rough-hewn and at times fervent manner. The Christianity he preached (literally preached: Drake loved to gather his crews on deck and treat them to his sermons) and practised was deeply patriotic and bellicose. A son of the still-recent Reformation, Drake was a Protestant – a "Lutheran", the Spanish called it – and while still young came to hate both the Pope installed in Rome and all the nations obedient to him, particularly Spain. To steal from Spanish ships was far from a violation of the Eighth Commandment: it was a blow struck against the secular enemy of England and against the Papal Antichrist.

In fact, Drake's whole dazzling career can be seen as a major chapter in two much bigger stories. The first was the state of covert and then open warfare between Spain and England, which ultimately led to the decline of the former and the triumph of the latter; the second was the conflict between the older forces of Catholic Christianity and the rising power of various modes of Protestantism across Europe. Two figures dominate these years: the pious Catholic Philip II of Spain and the stern if pragmatic protestant Elizabeth I of England. Philip regarded Elizabeth as a dangerous heretic who should be deposed as quickly as possible to return England to the Catholic faith (they were distantly related, and sometimes addressed each other in formal correspondence as "sister" and "brother"); Elizabeth was the daughter of Henry VIII, the Tudor king who had defied Rome, and one of her first actions after being crowned in 1558 was to establish an English church. Drake, only about 18 at the time of her Coronation, would ultimately become Elizabeth's most deadly weapon against Philip.

Driven by vengeful hate though he was, Drake nonetheless treated the Spanish he captured with a chivalrous generosity that would be unusual in any military leader, and was almost unknown in his own savage times. The noblemen he captured were first surprised, then entranced by the way he would treat them as honoured guests, entertaining them to lavish feasts and winning their affection with his frank and agreeable manners. He could be a harsh disciplinarian, and at one point executed a close friend found guilty of sedition; but those who visited his ships either willingly or under armed guard, usually reported that his men adored him.

Background and Early Years

There is no definite proof of Drake's date of birth; it was probably some time in the first two months of 1540, but it might have been as early as 1538 or as late as 1541. Francis was the first-born son of the family, and would eventually have no fewer than eleven younger brothers. His father's name was Edmund – we do not know his mother's name – and at the time of Francis' birth Edmund Drake and his wife were living near Plymouth in a labourer's cottage owned by his father. In later years, Edmund Drake became ordained as a Deacon. At some point in Francis' childhood, probably around 1549, the Drake family moved to Kent and for a while lived in picturesque style inside the upturned hull of a retired ship.

Francis was about 10 years old when his father apprenticed him to the owner of a small merchant ship that worked the English shoreline and sometimes crossed to

France. His captain, and thus first teacher of maritime skills, was an elderly man with no children of his own. We can assume that Francis was an apt pupil, since the historian William Camden reports that "the youth being painful [i.e., painstaking] and diligent, so pleased the old man by his industry, that being a bachelor, at his death he bequeathed his bark [boat] unto him by will and testament." This modest vessel was his first command.

By about 1564 or 1565, Francis appears to have joined a mission to the West Indies as second-in-command to one John Lovell. Not much is known about this voyage, except that Francis must have fallen briefly into the hands of the Spanish in Rio de la Hacha on the Isthmus of Panama – known to the English as the Spanish Main. He was treated badly by them in some unspecified way. One likely suggestion is that the local Treasurer insulted him and confiscated his goods. Whatever happened, Drake regarded the Spanish with hatred from this time onwards, and his vengefulness grew deeper with the passing years. He was convinced that he had been personally cheated, and for the rest of his life believed that he had personal as well as patriotic and religious justification for plundering any Spanish possessions.

After another short voyage, to the coast of Guinea, Francis returned to England in 1566 and went to see his distant relative, John Hawkins, a rich and powerful figure in the slave trade. This episode in Drake's early career is the one that rightly appals modern historians. Perhaps the only thing to be said is that Drake was very much a man of his age, and that almost no one save a few idealistic souls in France and England raised any moral objections to slavery at this time. Elizabeth herself invested in slaving expeditions, and profited by them.

John Hawkins took a shine to his young kinsman, and when, in October 1567, he sailed from England with a fleet of five ships, bound for Africa and the capture of slaves, he put one of them – a fifty-ton vessel named the *Judith* – under the command of Francis. This mission lasted about fifteen months, and was almost entirely disastrous.

The fleet ran into storms off Finisterre, and one of the ships, the *Jesus*, suffered such bad damage that Hawkins was on the point of deciding to abandon the whole enterprise and sail home. But the storms abated, and the fleet regrouped near Tenerife, before setting a course for the African coast. On the way, they captured two ships, one a Portuguese caravel, the other captained by a French pirate named Bland, who had only recently seized the vessel himself.

On arrival at the "hunting-ground" of the Guinea coast, the Englishmen met with more deadly resistance than they had expected. Instead of submitting meekly to captivity, the locals showered their would-be masters with arrows bearing a lethal poison. Anyone hit by such an arrow would die in agonies within ten days.

Though many of the English were killed or wounded, Hawkins was ready for a second strike. He managed to form an alliance with a local king who wanted to attack a rival in a nearby settlement; Hawkins and the king unleashed their combined forces. Hawkins' men took two hundred and fifty captives, while the King's forces took six hundred. Hawkins demanded that these six hundred should be handed over to him as the fee for his action, but – to the Englishman's indignation – the King marched them all away that night.

They sailed on to the West Indies, where they planned

to sell their slaves to the Spanish for a handsome profit. The first couple of stops were reasonably successful, but then they came to the place of Drake's recent humiliation: Rio de la Hacha. Accounts of what happened next do not tally, but the most likely account, and one in which we see for the first time the distinctive martial style of Francis Drake, maintains that Drake took the *Judith* and its companion ship the *Angel* into harbour ahead of the other ships as a deliberate act of provocation.

The Spanish were duly provoked, and fired on the English ships. Drake fired back, blowing a hole in the house of the Treasurer who had swindled him. Then Drake promptly seized a Spanish despatch boat. Hawkins and the rest of the fleet caught up with them, and, in face of heavy fire from some two hundred rifles, took control of the town and forced the Spanish about six miles out of town. Humiliated, they surrendered and came to terms with Hawkins. One of his conditions was that they should buy every last one of his slaves.

So far, a triumph for Drake. Hawkins, knowing that the storms season was almost on them, resolved to head back to England as quickly as possible. But an early storm damaged one of the ships, the *Jesus*, so severely that she could only be saved by putting back into shore. As they tried to do so, they met with three Spanish ships with about a hundred passengers. Hawkins took all of them hostage, and then sailed to an anchorage near Vera Cruz.

And it was here that they sighted twelve Spanish treasure ships, sailing far ahead of a heavily armed protective squadron of thirteen large ships that would accompany them back to Spain. The captains of the Spanish treasure vessels mistook the English fleet for one of their own, and came peaceably alongside. They were astonished when Hawkins, with extreme politeness, explained to them that the treasure ships were now his; he did not want to resort to arms, and required only to be left in peace and be helped with repairs, for which he would pay a fair price.

On the following morning, the thirteen armed ships also came alongside. Hawkins sent a flagship to repeat what he had told the treasure ship captains. After a certain amount of negotiation, the two sides each handed over twelve hostages, and the Spanish ships dropped anchor very close to the English ships. For three days, nothing happened, and the English busied themselves with repairs. It seemed too good to be true; and it was.

On a sudden command, armed Spanish troops poured out of the ships. One party raced ashore, and shot dead the unarmed English sailors. Others climbed on board the *Jesus* and the *Minion*. Then the cannon opened fire at close range. The *Angel* sank, and the *Jesus* and the *Swallow* were gravely damaged. Hawkins fought back with the ferocity of a man staring into the face of massacre. It was a brutal scene, and the Spanish took the worst of it: five hundred sailors dead, four of the thirteen ships sunk.

When he found that the *Jesus* could not be moved from its mooring, Hawkins ordered his men to abandon ship and regroup on the *Minion*. Since the *Minion* was already dangerously overcrowded, he told Drake to come alongside in the *Judith*, rescue as many men as he could, and then retreat out to open sea. Drake followed his command, and sailed away from harbour straight into a storm. By the time the storm had cleared, he was far away from the *Minion* and did not know whether he should risk staying close to the enemy in case Hawkins had managed to escape, or take the less risky option of saving as many Englishmen as he could by setting off home.

He chose the latter course, and has often been condemned for it. But Hawkins, who had survived the attack and sailed the *Minion* to a safe berth where she rode out the storm that had separated them, would never express any resentment at Drake's action. Drake had done what Hawkins himself would have done.

On 20 January 1569, the *Judith*, crammed with starving sailors, sailed alone into the harbour at Plymouth.

Chapter Four

Drake on the Spanish Main

D rake had sailed away from England penniless, and he returned penniless. Within six months of his return, his need to make money became all the more urgent: he married his Plymouth sweetheart, Mary Newman, on 4 July 1569. But, though he did not know it at the time, he brought back something that was extremely valuable to his monarch: news of the Spanish treachery.

While Drake had been away, England had entered into a new phase of its constantly mutating relationship with Spain. In November 1568, just two months earlier, a Spanish ship had taken refuge from French pirates in Plymouth. On board was no less than £100,000, most of it intended as payment for the Spanish troops stationed in the Netherlands under the Duke of Alva. Queen Elizabeth rightly saw Alva as a threat to her realm; she also loved money, and she confiscated the sum in the Tower of London for an indefinite period.

Alva was outraged, and, under orders from home,

took his revenge by putting an embargo on all English property in the Netherlands. The war of words became more intense. The Spanish ambassador was dismissed, and another Spanish diplomat placed under house arrest. So when Hawkins and Drake came to tell Elizabeth the bad news, she was secretly exultant. Now she could hold onto the money while playing the injured party. She may also have seen something potentially valuable in this man Drake, but he was still relatively young and untested.

For the next couple of years, Drake spent most of his time on discreet journeys of reconnaissance to the Spanish Main, "Main" meaning "mainland". This was the long stretch of eastern coastline, held by Spain, that ran from Florida to present-day Venezuela. Spanish ships sailed to and from the Main in the Gulf of Mexico and the Caribbean, which was why this area attracted so many pirates. Drake was probably funded by the Hawkins firm. On his first voyage in 1570, he took just two small ships, the *Dragon* and the *Swan*; for the second, in 1571, he took the *Swan* alone. What he was trying to discover was the viability of the routes by which gold and silver was brought from Peru and loaded on to ships bound for Spain. Drake wanted to see where the routes were most vulnerable to attack by land and sea.

Eventually, he came across a small natural harbour on the coast of Darien. He made a temporary base here, and named it Port Pheasant, after the abundance of that tasty and nutritious bird. Now he formed his master plan – or, at least, he dreamed of the main objective which he planned to achieve by whatever means he could improvise.

He had now seen the Spanish method of conveying precious metals. From the famous mines in Peru, they would make their way in mule trains across Panama to the city of Nombre de Dios, on the coast; or if the rivers were high enough, they would load rafts for the same destination. In each case, the panniers of treasure would be unloaded, and ton after ton of gold and silver put on board ships bound for Cadiz. This treasure was his new obsession.

His long reconnaissance complete, he began the trip back to England, finally allowing himself the luxury of taking a few ships; this time, he would not be coming home penniless.

Briefly reunited with his wife Mary, he brooded on the campaign ahead. He decided to adopt the most dangerous of strategies: to make a direct assault on Nombre de Dios, fight down the troops stationed there, and loot everything they could find in the treasure stores. Drake had such faith in his own powers and those of his men that he thought the feat could be carried out with just two ships – the small *Swan* and a much larger vessel of seventy tons, the *Pasha*. He recruited seventy-three young men and boys, most of them from Plymouth; two of them were his younger brothers, John and Joseph. Then he loaded the two ships with enough provisions for a year's voyage, and had three small pinnaces – swift, lightweight boats – taken apart and placed below deck for re-assembly on the other side of the ocean. These pinnaces were to prove invaluable.

They sailed on 24 May 1572, and headed directly back to Port Pheasant. Though the place had become over-grown in the months he had been back in England, he soon recognised it – but in a grim way. His stores cached there had been dug up and emptied; and he found a note attached to a tree. It was the work of his old shipmate John Garrett, who warned him to flee at once:

"Captain Drake. If you fortune to come
into this port make haste away: for the
Spaniards which you had with you here
last year have bewrayed [discovered] this
place, and taken away all that you left here.
I departed from hence this present 7th July,
1572. Your very loving friend, JOHN
GARRET."

7th July: just five days earlier.

Drake pondered the implications of this message. Should
he abandon this base as too dangerous, and build a new
one elsewhere? On reflection, he decided that it was quite
likely that the people who had stolen his stores would not
have known that they belonged to Drake and his English
crew. Instead of running, he set his seventy-three boys
and men to felling trees, and then building a high-walled
enclosure in the shape of a pentagon, covering about
three-quarters of an acre. The pinnaces were taken out and
re-assembled, ready for action.

While the work continued, they had an unexpected
visitor – not the enemy, but an English pirate ship, owned
by the veteran privateer Sir Edward Horsey and now
captained by one James Ranse – at almost forty, quite an
old man for the risky business of piracy. This ship had
just captured a small Spanish despatch boat and a shallop – a small open boat suitable for rowing or sailing in
shallow waters. Drake greeted Ranse politely, and outlined
his vision of an attack on Nombre de Dios. Ranse was
excited. He asked to join forces, and Drake, though
inwardly annoyed at this Johnny-come-lately, agreed to

accept him, on the condition that Drake should remain sole commander.

Drake decided that he could put the captured shallop to good use: like the pinnaces, it was light and swift. He manned it with twenty of Ranse's sailors. Then he assigned fifty-three of his own boys to the three pinnaces. They were armed with pikes, and tarred arrows that would be set on fire before being shot at the enemy. Drake, understanding the emotional power of music in stirring his own forces and frightening the opposing one, also issued them with drums and trumpets. And, as far as possible, he used a "buddy" system, which meant that best friends would be seated next to each other. Drake understood a truth that most military men would confirm: in the heat of battle, you fight not so much for Queen and Country as for your mates.

They set out westwards for Nombre de Dios, sailing when they could, rowing when the wind dropped. Their first encounter was undramatic but crucial. Putting in to shore at a place he called the "Isle of Pines", Drake spotted two Spanish frigates being loaded with timber. But the workers on land were not Spanish: they were Cimaroon slaves. Drake now came up with a stroke of diplomatic brilliance.

He talked with them in quiet, friendly and respectful terms, and soon learned how much they hated their Spanish captors. In fact, they had themselves tried to attack Nombre de Dios, but had been driven back by heavy gunfire. Drake offered them a safe conduct back to the mainland, where – he hoped – they would tell all their families how polite and gentle these English were, and how they hated the Spanish just as fiercely as the natives did. They accepted the offer with joy –and this is where and why the verb "to maroon" enters the English language, as the Cimaroons had been kidnapped and dumped on the island. Before long, Drake's policy would prove decisive.

It was time to launch the attack. Drake left the three main ships – the *Swan*, the *Pasha* and Ranse's craft – in hiding on the Isle of Pines. With the pinnaces and the shallop, they made their way stealthily along the coast, unseen by any Spanish vessels. By the last day of July, they had reached the eastern promontory of the bay on which Nombre de Dios was located. It was nightfall, and Drake had told his men that they would attack at dawn.

But as the hours of darkness passed, Drake noticed that his boys were growing nervous and uneasy. This was no way to begin a major assault, so when, at about three a.m. the moon rose and shone light down on the waters, Drake declared that it was officially dawn. The pinnaces glided around the promontory and into the bay – where, almost at once, they encountered the unexpected obstacle of a Spanish vessel that had just dropped anchor.

Drake ordered some of his men to take the Spanish boat, and the others to storm the fort. There was only one Spanish guard, and when he saw the English approach he raced into town to raise the alarm. Within a couple of minutes, the church bells were ringing out a warning, and the town was woken. They could have fired on the church tower, but Drake ordered them to hold their fire – not for pious reasons, but because they needed their muskets for more urgent and softer targets.

Leaving sixteen boys to guard the pinnaces in harbour, he divided his forces. John Oxenham, John Drake and their party would go round the outside of the town and then attack from the east, with the aim of seizing the Governor's mansion in the market square. Drake's force would simply march straight into town, with drum beating, trumpet blaring, and burning arrows ready to be shot. In the market square, they were met by a small band of musketeers, who shot his trumpeter dead while Drake sustained a serious leg wound. The enemies began to fight at close range, with pikes and swords.

But now John Drake's men came in to the square from the east, and let fly more volleys of flaming arrows. The Spanish panicked, and fled. Nombre de Dios belonged to Drake. He ordered some of the Spanish prisoners they had just taken to lead them to the store-room of the Governor's house. What they saw there, by the light of their torches, was a spectacle that might dazzle any European monarch, yet alone young lads from Devon. Twelve feet high, ten feet thick and seventy feet long was a wall made up entirely of silver bars. The boys were astonished; but Drake did not allow them to waste time in gaping at the sight.

He suspected that there was gold as well as silver in this town, and his guess was that it was in a Treasury building near the harbour. He sent his brother and Oxenham ahead to investigate, and organised the boys into an armed guard to protect the wall of silver. Just at this moment of triumph, fate turned against them.

First, a violent thunderstorm put paid to any serious movement for more than half an hour. Then, in the middle of giving his boys a rousing speech, Drake made faint by loss of his blood, dropped to the floor. Up to this point, he had made such a stoical show that no one was aware he had been. But now everyone could see the blood seeping from his leg wound. They bound it and stopped the bleeding, and tried to revive him with some brandy. They begged him to abandon the mission and come back to the pinnaces, but he stubbornly refused. Then – in an act of mutiny which was in reality an act of love – they lifted him up and carried him back to the pinnaces. Drake mattered more to them than gold and silver.

And so this daring coup came to nothing. There would be time for a more profitable raid on Nombre de Dios soon enough; for now, they must retreat before Spanish reinforcements arrived. And though they had taken no treasure, they did not come away entirely empty-handed; just before leaving the bay, they relieved the Spanish ship of its generous stores of Canary wine. By the time the sun rose, they had rowed into a small island out of the range of gunshot, and rested there for a few days. They named it the Victualling Island. No one said anything about a court martial for mutiny.

While they nursed their wounds, a curiously courte-ous incident took place. Showing a flag of truce, a young Spanish officer sailed over to parley with them. Drake agreed to an interview. Ostensibly, the young man was here to determine the full strengths of the two bands of men that had created such havoc, and to ask whether the arrows used by the English had been steeped in poison. But what he was most eager to learn was whether their captain was this "Drake" who had been skulking around their possessions for the past couple of years.

Drake reassured him that the English never used poison arrows, and admitted, not without vanity, that he was indeed their increasingly well-known enemy. Then – again, very much in character – he ordered a lavish meal, well lubricated with fine Canary, and accompanied by the strains of his musicians. The young officer later spoke admiringly of Drake's remarkable generosity and good spirits, and said that he had never been so honoured in his life.

But it was obviously time to part, before their guest could make it known how small their forces actually were. The next morning, they set back for Isle of Pines. When the two commanders met, Captain Ranse told Captain Drake that their cover had been blown, and that the risk now involved in staging raids was unacceptably high. Drake made a show of agreeing, and Ranse sailed his ship and men away.

What next? Drake still needed to recover from his wound, so he sent John Drake and another crewman, Ellis Hixom, off on a single pinnace to make another reconnaissance trip to the River Chagres, where the Spanish would sometimes load treasure on to ships bound for Nombre de Dios. While he rested, Drake came up with his next ploy. Though his intention was to attack the treasure trains by land, he wanted the Spanish to think that he was still set on attacking them by sea. So he organised what was in effect a giant feint: he would seem to be staging a massive attack on the port of Cartagena.

Cartagena was, he knew, far too well defended to be taken by their modest forces; but he knew that he could taunt and scare the town without too much risk. So he sailed his three pinnaces into the harbour there at nightfall, and found a single Spanish frigate there, with a crew of just one: a talkative and possibly slightly demented old man. The old man greeted them cheerfully, and told them that they were in luck – a big ship from Seville had just unloaded in the next bay along the coast.

This offered the chance for a major prank. Drake's three ships promptly found the Spanish vessel; crept on board and locked down the hatches while the sailors were all asleep; and then set up a tow-rope. When the sun was fully up, they towed the ship right across the main harbour, in plain sight of the town. The alarm went up, and the cannon on shore began to fire at them, but they were just beyond range. They sailed back to the Isle of Pines with their new prize, setting its crew ashore on a smaller island on the way.

Drake had one more problem to solve before he could move on to the next phase of his campaign. He now no longer had sufficient crew to man both the pinnaces and the two big ships. He considered leaving one of the big ships behind, but an unmanned ship would soon fall into the hands of the Spanish and be used against him. He would have to sacrifice one of the ships, and that ship must be the *Swan*, since only the *Pasha* was large enough to hold all his men and to function as a base.

But this drastic move posed problems of loyalty and morale. His brother John was now the captain of the *Swan*, and would bitterly resent having the command taken out of his hands. John Drake's crew, in the way of sailors when they have seen action in their craft, were also deeply loyal to the *Swan*.

It had to be done by subterfuge. Drake summoned his carpenter, Thomas Moone, and ordered him to secretly board the *Swan* that night, and to bore three holes in the hull, near to the keel – small enough not to allow the incoming water to make a boiling noise, wide enough that the boat would surely sink in a matter of hours. Moone bridled at the order, but relented when Drake explained his intentions.

By the next morning, Drake had come to see the humorous side of this tactic. He sailed over to the *Swan* on a pinnace, and innocently invited John to come on an agreeable fishing trip. John duly joined him, and as they sailed away, Drake feigned surprise that the *Swan* was riding unusually low in the water. John was alarmed, and shouted out to the steward to check below deck. Sure enough, the hold was about waist-deep in water. John was anxious to get back on board at once, but Drake persuaded him that all he needed to do was set men pumping. He should relax, let his crew do the hard work, and enjoy the fishing.

While the brothers fished, the crew pumped and pumped, well into the late afternoon. Their efforts seemed futile – no matter how hard they worked, the ship continued slowly to sink… By the time John and Francis Drake returned, it was clear that the *Swan* was doomed. All Drake could advise was to have the crew rescue their belongings, and then set fire to the ship so that she could never be raised again by the enemy.

John Drake was distraught, and Francis comforted him by telling him that he should now command the *Pasha*. Drake himself would stay with the pinnaces until they found a new prize.

It was now the middle of August, and Drake had successfully cleared the last obstacle to starting his campaign. No one suspected his hand in the sinking, and by the time the secret was uncovered, no one greatly cared. From now on, his target was the land route along which the Spanish carried their treasures.

Chapter Five

The Treasure Trains

D rake sailed up the Gulf of Darien, hid the *Pasha* in an inlet, and politely asked the local Cimaroons to build him a village in their traditional style. This would serve as a secure headquarters for his actions. While the Cimaroons worked, he gave his men a rest break: he divided them into two teams, each of which would labour while the other played bowls and quoits and other games. "Work" for the Englishmen consisted largely of hunting, fishing and foraging – despite the heat and humidity, not too arduous a task, since the lands, skies and waters were rich in prey.

From this secure base, Drake set out on some minor raids with two swift pinnaces, mostly in search of supply vessels which would yield maize, pigs and other useful goods. In more peaceful spirit, he sent men to gather fresh vegetables from the nearby island of Tolou. Behind these necessary tasks was a long-term stratagem. As with his feint at Cartagena, Drake wanted his raids to be known about, so that the Spanish would make the assumption that he was set on purely maritime attacks, and so divert their forces to deal with him on the east coast. But his intention was to make his next great raid by land.

He chose to sail with the raiding parties, and now spent several weeks at sea, repeatedly slipping through the traps which the Spanish fleet laid for them. At one point, they tried to tempt Drake by sending an apparently empty frigate out to sea, with soldiers hidden below deck, but Drake saw through the trick. On another occasion, he jumped ashore and yelled his defiance at any Spanish troops that might be hiding in the forests. He wanted his boys, especially, to feel that they were taking part in a great adventure.

It might well have worked perfectly had the weather not been against him. The longer they remained out at sea, the more his boys began to suffer ill health from exposure to extremes of heat by day and cold by night. He relented, and sailed back to the base camp so that they could recover in relative comfort.

There was bad news. Drake had skilfully avoided Spanish lures, but others had not. Out at sea one day, the crew of a pinnace commanded by John Drake spotted a frigate that might easily be taken. John Drake refused to give chase, as they had only a few swords and guns with them, but his men jeered at him for being a coward. John grew angry, and put himself at the bow of his pinnace for the attack. He had been right to be cautious: the frigate was full of men armed with pikes. After a brief skirmish, the English made a hurried retreat, but they lost two men, including John Drake.

This was a grave blow, and worse was to come. In January 1573, the camp was struck by a serious illness; probably yellow fever. Within a couple of days six men had died; within a few more, thirty – almost half the company. Among the dead was Joseph Drake, who died in his brother's arms. What Drake did next has been greeted with dismay and even disgust by some historians: he ordered the doctor to dissect the fresh corpse to see what organs the mysterious disease affected. From our perspective, it seems clear enough that Drake was simply putting aside his personal sentiments for the greater good. Whatever his intentions, the act was futile. The doctor found nothing that might suggest a cure. In desperation, the doctor then put together a powerful drug that might, he hoped, act as a drastic cure. It killed him.

Morale was sinking fast, but there was one hopeful sign, and Drake was encouraged by it. The bonds of friendship between the Indians and the Englishman had by now grown strong, and the Indians declared themselves more than willing to join in attacks on their common enemy, the Spanish. They matched words with actions by sending scouts, who soon discovered that the fleet which had arrived to collect treasure for Spain at this time of year had just sailed in to Nombre de Dios. Drake sent a pinnace out to reconnoitre, and his men confirmed the report.

It was time for action. Though Drake realized that too many of his men were seriously ill to take part in his mission, he managed to put together a raiding party of forty-eight men in sound health: eighteen English, thirty Cimaroon. He ordered Ellis Hixom to stay behind at the base, to tend the sick and protect their ship and pinnaces. Drake cautioned him not to trust any orders that might come to him unless they came with his own signature.

And so Drake and his squad set off deep into the interior, in search of the treasure trains.

On 11 February, they caught sight of the peak where Balboa had once stood, and climbed eagerly towards it. Just a few hours later Drake enjoyed his vision of the Pacific Ocean – a single moment of revelation that changed both his life and the course of history.

It took another march of two days to bring them out of the pine forest and into open ground – low hills, thickly covered with pampas grass, and leading down into a plain. They marched for another two days, catching glimpses now and then of the city of Panama as they walked over the tops of hills. Finally, just three miles outside town, Drake called a halt and sent scouts ahead to find out news about the movements of treasure.

The news was good: there would be two trains setting out that night, carrying food and other supplies but also plenty of silver, gold and jewels. Drake planned out his attack, which would take place at night, when the mule trains travelled to avoid the searing daytime heat. He retraced their steps, and halted again about six miles outside Vera Cruz, at a suitable point for ambush. He told his men to eat, enjoy a tot of brandy, and then ordered them to take off their shirts and wear them over their coats, so that they should be able to tell friend from enemy in the darkness. The mules duly came, and the men pounced.

The results were farcical. While the mules were still a fair distance away, a horseman unexpectedly galloped past them from the direction of Vera Cruz. One of his younger boys, Robert Pike – who had clearly enjoyed his ration of brandy too much – broke his General's orders and jumped valiantly up for the attack. A Cimaroon dragged him back down and sat on him, but the damage was done. The horseman had seen him, and continued swiftly on his way.

Before long, loaded mules came into sight. Drake whistled for action, and his men raced down to ambush. But the muleteers put up no resistance, and Drake soon found out why. The horseman had warned the mule train of their plans, and its leader had ordered all the treasure back into Panama. These captured mules carried nothing but provisions.

Drake conferred with Pedro, who set out two alternatives: either to go back into the forest and make a long circuit round Vera Cruz, or adopt the more drastic option of trying to storm right through it. Knowing that his men were weary, Drake immediately decided on the quicker, more hazardous choice. They began their march on Vera Cruz immediately. When they were within a mile of the town, they were challenged by a Spanish guard. Drake demanded passage in the name of Elizabeth. They responded with gunfire, slightly wounding Drake and killing one of his men.

This was unbearable provocation for the Cimaroons, who charged the guard and chased them off, then led the English on a violent passage through the town. Terrified, the inhabitants all fled their houses and barracks and took shelter together in the monastery. In one of his shows of ostentatious chivalry, Drake assured them that he would make sure that they came to no harm. He kept his word, and on the very next morning, the small army set out on a weary march back to their ship. He sent an envoy ahead, carrying orders to Hixom that they should all rendezvous at the mouth of the river Tortugas.

His messenger carried out the task to the letter, but Hixom looked on him suspiciously, remembering Drake's warnings about the possibility of faked orders. Now, the Cimaroon handed Hixom a golden toothpick. Hixom was baffled; was this some kind of trap? But the Cimaroon pointed at the toothpick, gesturing that Hixom should examine it more closely. He examined its handle, and saw words in a handwriting he recognised: "By me, Francis Drake" All was well, and he followed his orders.

When the wearied marchers finally reached the anchorage, their spirits rose. The sickness had gone, and the survivors were not only healthy but eager for more adventure. So far, they had almost nothing to show for their pains, and though the temptation to cut their losses and return home empty-handed was tempting for the exhausted, most of the company were keen to go back to the treasure-hunt. Drake listened to their proposals, and then decided on action. They would begin minor raids by sea again, partly in the genuine hope of prizes, but also to make the Spanish even more certain that he had now abandoned a short-lived policy of raids by land and returned to his traditional methods as a pirate. Besides, his men were ravenous for the proper food that a Spanish supply ship would carry.

Within a few days, they had made their first conquest – a new and generously laden Spanish frigate. They put its crew in one of the ship's own boats, and sent them off to shore, then brought it back to their anchorage, where the hungry men feasted on its rich provisions. It happened to be Eastertide, and Drake let his men celebrate while he had the new frigate prepared for his own purposes. The next day, he took it for a trial run.

Their first encounter took them by surprise. The large ship they sighted proved to be not Spanish but French, under the command of one captain Testu. The French seemed harmless, and were suffering badly from lack of fresh water and food. Drake took them back and invited them aboard the *Pasha*, where he talked and negotiated with the French captain. It was here that Drake heard about the atrocity which had horrified all Protestant Europe – the massacre of Huguenots in France a few months earlier.

For six days, Drake allowed his new French friends to recover from their starvation. While they recovered, he plotted a new exploit – an exceptionally daring one, to be carried out in partnership with the Frenchmen they had rescued. He would make a second attempt on the treasure trains, this time near Nombre de Dios. While this was attempted, the *Pasha* and the French ship should remain in hiding. He sailed in the captured Spanish frigate with two pinnaces in support.

His initial plan was to land in the mouth of the Rio Francisco, about twenty miles from Nombre de Dios. But the waters proved too difficult, so once again he was forced to improvise. He sent men ashore aboard the pinnaces, with orders that those left on board should hide themselves for four days and then make for a rendezvous point.

Captain Testu had misgivings. He doubted that they would ever see the pinnaces again; he feared that the Cimaroons, though ferociously loyal to their English friends, would happily kill his own men; and may well have been frightened when he learned the precise details of Drake's plan of battle, which to more cautious souls looked foolhardy to the point of insanity.

Drake's plan was a gamble for high stakes. Where almost any other commander would have planned to attack the incoming mule trains when they were far from help, Drake intended to let them come to within a mile of Nombre de Dios, and strike them just at the point where they would start to think that they were out of danger. Surprise was the key.

Since the raiding party had landed to the east of Nombre de Dios, and Drake planned to attack near its western gate, he had to make a long detour, staying well hidden in the forest – a distance of about twenty miles in difficult terrain. At this season, the heat of the day was so intense that the Spanish slept during the hours of sunlight and only woke up to work at dusk. By the end of the second day, Drake's men were in place and waiting. They did not have long to wait.

Early the next day, just before dawn, scouts reported that no fewer than three trains were approaching: a total of one hundred and ninety mules, each one labouring under a hefty weight of gold and silver, and guarded by forty-five armed soldiers. Within an hour, Drake's men could hear the sound of tinkling bells from the approaching train. It grew louder and louder, and finally the train came into sight. Drake held his men back until their prey was in just the right position, and then he whistled for an attack. The combined English, Cimaroon and French forces jumped out of the bushes.

They met with only brief resistance. Scouts seized hold of the very first and the very last mules in the train, and all of the animals in between lay down obediently, as they had been trained to do whenever a halt was called. One of the Cimaroons was shot dead, and Captain Testu sustained a serious wound in his stomach, but then the Spanish soldiers fled, to call for reinforcements in Nombre de Dios. The raiders ripped open the panniers, and were dumbfounded by the vast quantities of treasure they found.

Their haul was so rich that it soon became obvious they could not possibly carry it back with them. Instead, they separated all the silver from the gold, and buried the silver – some thirty tons of it, they estimated – in various hiding places near a local river. Then, each man burdened with pounds of gold, they set off back into the forest as quickly as they could. Already, they could hear the noise of a mounted force on its way from the town.

Once in the forest, Captain Testu told Drake that he was too seriously wounded to make the march. He asked to be left behind with two of his own men to guard him, in the hope of recovering sufficiently well to catch up. Drake agreed, and promised that if Testu were not up to the trip, he would send a rescue party for him and his guards.

For the next two days, Drake and his men made painfully slow progress through the woods, sweating profusely in the terrible heat. Then, on their second night of marching, a tremendous storm blew up, and battered them with wind and rain. They slid and fell in the mud, and their slow walk grew even slower. It was not until the late afternoon of the fourth day that they reached their rendezvous at the river.

Disaster. There were no pinnaces to be seen. What *could* be seen, out at sea and apparently sailing directly towards them, were Spanish ships. Drake mulled over the possibilities. What seemed most likely was that the Spanish had captured their pinnaces; and possibly the frigate as well. And even if the frigate had survived, her draught was too deep for her to able to sail near the coast. If all this was indeed the case, their position was desperate – trapped between Spanish ships ahead of them and Spanish troops behind.

It was the most dangerous moment of Drake's life so far, and he reacted to it in a manner which became part of his legend. Looking at the river, he saw that it was full of broken wood – branches and trunks and whole trees, smashed apart by the recent storm and now being washed out to sea. Drake let out a joyous yelp, and told his men and boys that these lumps of wood were "offering themselves" to be made into a raft. He would put out to sea, and try to find his frigate in the bay where it might well be anchored.

The company jumped into the river and began to drag the broken trees up onto the riverbank. They chopped and assembled and lashed the wood together, working furiously through the night. By dawn, they had fashioned a small, crude but navigable raft, with a mast – an old biscuit sack was fixed to it by way of a sail – four oars and a rudder. It could, at a pinch, carry four passengers. Or so they hoped.

Leading by example, Drake insisted that he should be one of the quartet to test her. He was joined by one of his Devonshire boys, and by two Frenchmen with a reputation for being strong swimmers. They stepped on board, and the raft sank below the water under their combined weight. But it did not sink entirely, so they set to with the oars and paddled away. As they left, Drake turned around to shout a message of cheer: with God's help, he would find the frigate and "get them all aboard in spite of all the Spaniards in the Indes!"

Once they were in open water, they were in even greater peril of sinking. When high waves splashed over them, the waters came up as high as their chests and even their necks. The sun was intense, and the salt spray soon made their skins crack. They rowed on and on, for six hours, until finally the burning sun began to set and they finally felt cool again. But an easterly wind sprang up against them, and slowed them to the point where they could barely tell if they were moving forward at all.

Finally, their luck turned. Through the twilight, Drake could see two spots on the horizon. He urged his three companions to further efforts, and before long recognised his own pinnaces. He tore down the sack-mast and waved it in their air, screaming himself hoarse to alert their friends. But they were still too far off, and the pinnaces sailed out of sight behind a headland.

Drake guessed rightly that they were putting ashore for the night. He ordered his men to row straight at the land mass ahead of them, and they crashed awkwardly ashore. Drake's energy, always impressive, now astounded his men. Despite the four days of marching through the forest, the night constructing the raft and the painful hours of rowing it, he now insisted that they all run, not walk, across the hills of this promontory to meet the pinnaces: in fact, "he so willed the other three with him, as if they had been chased by the enemy".

Just as he had guessed, the pinnaces were at anchor ahead of them. He shouted a greeting, and was soon deep in conference with his captains. The explanation for their failure to make the rendezvous was simple: they had met with strong winds from the west, and simply could not make progress against it.

Now it was time for one of those practical jokes that so tickled Drake's boyish sense of humour. When the captains asked how their venture had gone, he pulled a long face and said, in lugubrious tones, "Well." This was exactly the kind of stoical response they would expect of him when times were bad, and they fell into a rueful silence. After a minute or so, they began to notice that Drake's long face had now broken into a grin. He brought out from his pocket "... a quoit of gold, thanking God that our voyage was made". They would be going back to England as rich men.

But before they could sail homewards, they must rescue their shipmates. Drake immediately ordered the pinnaces to sail back up the river and gather the men waiting there – as well, of course, as all the gold. Well before dawn, he had everyone and everything safely aboard. They sailed down the river and found the frigate safely in hiding. Then they returned to base, where they unpacked all their loot, divided the silver from the gold, and shared it out equally between the French and the English parties.

There was one outstanding duty before they could make their escape. Captain Testu and his men needed to be rescued. Once again, Drake insisted that he be part of the taskforce, and he took command until they came close to Nombre de Dios. Here, his men once again staged an affectionate act of mutiny, and said that they did not want their beloved Captain to go back into such hazardous places. He gave in gracefully, and handed command of the party to John Oxenham. On his return, he brought back just one French soldier; Testu and his other guard had been captured and interrogated. Then they were beheaded.

They returned to base, where Drake ordered the *Pasha* broken up, and put everyone on board the handsome frigate. The last thing he needed to do was to stock up with plenty of provisions for the weeks they would be on the ocean. A Spanish supply ship would be just the thing, and he knew where he could probably find one – at the port of Magdalena. To reach it, they had to sail again past Cartagena, where a substantial Spanish fleet was in dock. Almost every other captain in the world would have opted to set a course safely out to sea, and beyond enemy sight, but that was not Drake's style. Instead, he had the ship decked out in colourful silks, and flew the red and white Cross of St George from the maintop. He sailed closely past the Spanish fleet, in a gesture compounded of arrogance and contempt. Astonishingly, they were not pursued.

The very next morning, Drake spotted just the kind of supply ship he needed, and promptly captured it. It was brimming with high-quality foodstuffs and live animals, including honey, chicken, pigs. Then he sailed the two ships to a hiding place in the nearby islands. Here, they rested for a week, preparing for the Atlantic crossing by transferring provisions from their latest prize to the frigate and careening it – that is to say, tipping it on its side so as to scrape off the weed and barnacles that would slow it down, and – more urgent still – stripping off the marine worms and other parasites that might eat through the planks and riddle them with holes. Since the pinnaces were too small and fragile for a transatlantic trip, Drake ordered them to be broken up, and handed their ironwork over to the Cimaroons by way of a farewell present. He also had some more attractive gifts in mind.

Drake laid out a variety of goods for their choosing, including fine linen and silk for their wives. Pedro hankered for a scimitar which Drake had been given by captain Testu, but he was too shy to ask for it directly. Instead, he told one of his men to drop a few heavy hints about how much he desired the sword, and Drake gladly gave it to him, "with very good words". In return, Pedro gave Drake four more pieces of gold.

Before departure, they killed some two hundred and fifty turtles, and salted their delicious flesh for the journey home.

It was a swift journey, with favourable winds, and it took only twenty days for them to pass the Isles of Scilly. They arrived at Plymouth on the morning of Sunday, 4 August, 1573. They were sighted, and the exciting news spread along the coast. Contemporary reports tell the story of a distressed local preacher, who was giving a sermon to his congregation when a man ran in and whispered news that Drake's ships had come to harbour. The whispers spread right down through the pews, and within minutes all the worshippers had run out of the church and down to the quayside, where they greeted Drake and his crew with cheers and shouts of excitement. The preacher brought the service to an end on his own, and then ran outside to join his flock.

Drake had returned as a conquering hero. This was the start of his fame.

Chapter Six

Circumnavigation: Plotting the Course

I t was only a matter of days before the whole nation had heard of Drake's exploits, and rejoiced in the thrilling news. He was hailed on all sides as a new national hero, admired by the masses for his recklessness and verve, by patriots for having so marvellously trounced the enemy, by ardent protestants for having sorely offended the Pope, and – by the few thoughtful souls who cared about such things – for the humanity with which he had treated his prisoners. Drake had every cause to be pleased with his private life, too. Now wealthy, he had finally freed himself from dependence on the Hawkins family. He used some of his winnings to buy a house in Plymouth, near the Guildhall. He also bought three small ships, and ran them at a profit. A less driven man might have rested on his laurels; but Drake still seethed with ambition.

There was just one blemish on his new-found status as his country's hero. Elizabeth and her ministers could not be seen to approve of Drake's pillages. While Drake had been away, the Queen had tried to negotiate a more amicable settlement between England and Spain; there had even been talk of their joining forces as a superpower. It was while these delicate conversations with the Spanish Ambassador in London were taking place that Drake came back loaded with his booty.

So the Queen had put on a grand show of knowing absolutely nothing about his raids, even while she secretly exulted just as much as her subjects. Elizabeth could see that Drake might prove to be a great weapon in her long-term plan to challenge her "brother" Philip, but she also recognised that the time was not ripe to deploy him openly. So she sent a message to Drake, urging him to make himself scarce until a more propitious time. He dutifully disappeared for eighteen months.

Histories written not long after the event say that Drake promptly went to Ireland. Modern historians tend to agree, though there have been arguments about the precise dates. He may first have been sent on a brief mission escorting English merchant ships on the North Sea. The historian Stow says that "immediately on his return he furnished at his own expense, three frigates with men and munitions, and served voluntary in Ireland under Walter Earl of Essex where he did excellent service."

We have no records of how Drake regarded Essex's campaign in Ireland, but in the light of his own humane conduct with enemies it is likely that he regarded the savagery of the Earl's tactics as repugnant. Charged with putting down rebellious locals, Essex and his men conducted something closer to an indiscriminate massacre. In July 1575, for example, one of his generals – John Norreys – put ashore on Rathlin Island, where a party of Scottish soldiers and civilians had landed. The Scottish surrendered, but Norreys had all of them, children included, put to death. Essex communicated the news of this "triumph" to Elizabeth with immense satisfaction. Elizabeth, who could be terrifyingly callous even about the sufferings of her own sailors, was said to be pleased at the atrocity.

Fortunately for Drake's admirers, he took no direct part in these bloodbaths. His work was at sea – attacking both Spanish and Scottish frigates off the Irish coast, and sometimes transporting new forces for the Earl. It was during his time in Ireland that he met Captain Thomas Doughty, and formed a close friendship that just a few years later would become a dangerous enmity. Drake, who sometimes allowed his native right-headedness to be swayed when he met a fine gentleman, was utterly charmed by Doughty – an elegantly dressed, highly educated fellow who had been a lawyer at the Temple in London and was a scholar of both Ancient Greek and Hebrew.

After a final massacre in 1575, the Irish campaign came to an end, and Drake could again go home to Plymouth. Here, he discovered that his old friend John Oxenham, with whom he had shared his vision in Darien, had grown tired of waiting for Drake to organise a voyage, and was about to set off on a mission of his own. He raised funds for two ships and fifty-seven sailors, and they left England in April 1576. In later years, Drake learned that the trip had ended in disaster. Oxenham had sailed to Panama, recruited the same friendly Cimaroons they had met there, and built a ship on a river, along which he sailed until he came into the Southern Sea – and was thus the first Englishman ever to command a ship on the Pacific.

At first, Oxenham triumphed. He carried out raid after raid on Spanish vessels and loaded his ships with stolen treasure. But when he came back to land, Spanish troops were waiting for him. Oxenham's party came under heavy fire; all his men either fled, or were shot down, or taken prisoner. Eighteen men survived, and were brought as captives to Panama, where a dozen of them were hanged. Three boys were spared, and the last three men – Oxenham one of the trio – were put into the hands of the inquisition for the next two years. In 1580, they too were executed.

Before he had taken matters into his own hands, Oxenham had always said that Drake was the best man to take on the great task of invading the Pacific. Drake was never given to false modesty, and he agreed. In the comfort of his Plymouth house, he began to formulate his great idea. Circumnavigation of the world was almost certainly not part of his original plan. Drake's ambition was much simpler. All he really wanted was simply to sail into the Pacific via the Straits of Magellan, and attack the Spanish ships and settlements on and off the west coast of South America. Above all, he wanted to bring home vast quantities of Spanish booty, both to enrich himself and to win the enduring favour of the Queen.

Though a rich man, he was still not rich enough to finance such an exploit from his own purse. He formed a small syndicate of investors, and put £1,000 of his own into the pot. His first partners were Sir William Winter, who contributed £750, and his brother George, who gave £500. John Hawkins also gave £500. With the help of Doughty, he then began to seek patronage from some of the most powerful men in the country, as well as the most powerful woman.

In this long campaign of persuasion, Drake – unwisely – rested complete confidence in his new friend Doughty, who began his campaign to woo Elizabeth to their side by discreetly approaching Francis Walsingham. Now in his mid-forties, Walsingham was a shrewd politician who had risen rapidly up the ladder of politics under Elizabeth's reign, and was now Joint Principal Secretary of State. (In our own century, he is most frequently remembered as the master of Elizabeth's impressive and far-reaching Secret Service.) Walsingham was also fiercely hostile to Spain, and was pleased by Drake's record of attacks on the nation he regarded as England's worst enemy. He was also devoted to the notion that England should develop into a major sea power, first to rival and then to exceed Spain and Portugal.

Walsingham summoned Drake for an interview, and asked the mariner what he had in mind. Drake's replies impressed him so much that Walsingham then invited Drake to outline the details of his proposed voyage with a set of maps, and also to sign a statement of his aims and intentions. Drake refused the latter demand. What if the Queen – God Save Her! – should die while he was away at sea, and the country have a new monarch whose sympathies were with Spain? The fate of Sir Walter Raleigh shows that this was by no means an unreasonable anxiety. In 1618, Raleigh was executed at the command of James I, so as to appease Spain for the action of his troops in Venezuela, where they had ransacked a Spanish fort. Walsingham relented on this point, and went to inform Elizabeth.

Walsingham's enthusiasm for Drake's venture was matched by that of Robert Dudley, Earl of Leicester. A swashbuckling figure, who had come very close to marrying Elizabeth (she had been smitten by him, and he remained a favourite), Leicester was also bellicose about Spain. Both Leicester and Walsingham pressed Drake's cause with intense determination. And another highly influential noblemen soon joined them: the Earl of Lincoln, Christopher Hatton.

It is more than likely that Drake would also have been brought together with one of the most brilliant men of his age – Dr John Dee: the Welsh-born mathematician, navigator, geographer, astrologer (he had advised Elizabeth on the most auspicious day for her coronation), necromancer and leading theorist of British Maritime Expansion. He may have been the first writer ever to use the term "British Empire"; and if he was not literally the first, was at any rate the first to use it in front of his monarch.

Dee was on very good terms with both Leicester and Hatton, to which latter Dee had dedicated his book *The Perfect Art of Navigation*. Dee also knew the influential City of London merchant Richard Haklyut, a fellow Welshman whose cousin would one day write an important short history of Drake's circumnavigation. Dee held a series of conferences at his home in Mortlake, to the west of London, to which he invited those members of Court who shared his interest in global exploration and conquest.

Before Drake came on the scene with a plot that coincided at many points with their own, Dee and his colleagues had discussed several possible leaders of a British expedition south. The most obvious candidates were otherwise engaged. Walter Raleigh was, at twenty-three, considered too young; besides, at this time he was preoccupied with the eastern seaboard of North America. John Hawkins had been charged with the task of building up

Elizabeth's navy. Martin Frobisher was planning explorations in the cold seas to the north of America. And so on. And then they learned of this new hero, Drake...

In their early discussions, Drake had at least to give the impression that he was ready to fall in with the plans of his potential backers. Their ambitions varied greatly. Some were keenly interested in opening up an immensely profitable trade agreement with the Spice Islands – the Moluccas – and thus breaking Portugal's monopoly there. Others, like Sir Richard Greville, had for some time been advocating the foundation of British colonies in South America, to challenge the Spanish possessions in that continent.

Meanwhile, Dee and others urged that a British expedition should be sent in search of a place they called "Beach", or *Terra Australis Incognita*, which Marco Polo had described as a warm land where lumps off gold lay around on beaches, waiting to be picked up. (Drake was to discover, entirely by accident, that "Beach" – assumed to be a continuation of South America down towards the Pole – did not exist outside books.) Dee seems also to have nursed ambitions about taking the whole eastern seaboard of North America – he called it "Atlantis" – which he believed to have been claimed for Britain by one of his ancestors, the Welsh explorer-prince Owen Madoc, in 1170 AD.

Despite this confusion of motives, things were starting to look promising. But Drake also had a powerful opponent. Lord Burleigh, the nation's Lord Treasurer and the second most powerful person in England, was doggedly opposed to all English acts of piracy, and insisted that they were the most dangerous obstacle to securing a mutually beneficial peace treaty with Spain. The Secretary of State,

Walsingham, believed that no such treaty would ever be signed, and urged Elizabeth to prepare for an inevitable war with Philip.

As so often, Elizabeth vacillated hopelessly between the policies put forward by her advisors, torn by anxiety and avarice.

Both Drake and Doughty were well aware of Elizabeth's political dilemma. Secretly, she wished to inflict as much damage on Philip as was possible without provoking open warfare. She was also greedy for Philip's riches. But she knew how powerful the Spanish navy was, and she feared it. For the two decades that led up to the battle with the Spanish Armada in 1588, her standard policy was to deny all knowledge of English raids on Spanish ships and possessions.

But, to Drake's good fortune, Spanish foreign policy had just become more aggressive. Elizabeth had been negotiating a delicate settlement in the contested territory of the Netherlands. She was hoping for a compromise which would put strict limits on Spain's control over the country, but allow Philip enough of a military presence there to fend off possible invasion by France. Instead, Spain's governor in the Netherlands, Don John of Austria, had been taking bloody and punitive measures against its people; and it was rumoured that when he had subdued the Netherlands, his next target would be England.

Her rage became more powerful than her misgivings, and at last she agreed to a meeting with Drake. According to Drake's later account of the meeting – probably not altogether accurate – she shouted at him: "Drake! So it is that I would gladly be revenged on the King of Spain for divers injuries that I have received. You are the only man who may do this exploit. What is your advice?" He claimed that she gave him her full approval for raiding Spanish ships in the Pacific, and gave him an encouraging if modest sum of a thousand crowns – a crown being worth five shillings, or a quarter of a pound – by way of investment.

There were provisos. Elizabeth refused his request to borrow one of her ships, the *Swallow*, and she was adamant that he should maintain the fiction that she knew nothing of his plans. And she insisted that Burleigh, who would violently oppose the mission, must be kept completely in the dark about it. Finally, in a moment of uncharacteristic heartiness, she slapped Drake on the back and told him that he was the only one of her subjects who could pull off such an audacious scheme.

Drake immediately began to put together his fleet. He recruited volunteers from Plymouth and London, advertising both for mariners and for the soldiers he needed to fight on land. Activity on such a grand scale could not be kept secret: Antonio Senor de Guaras, Spain's diplomatic agent in London, could see that something significant was happening. He sent home the contrived rumour that "Drake the pirate is to go to Scotland with some little vessels for the purpose of getting possession of the Prince of Scotland."

When the gossip about Scotland died away, the next story to be put about was that Drake was simply arranging a peaceful trade mission to Alexandria. It was on this understanding that he had hired his crewmen – quite a gamble, since it opened up the possibility that the sailors would mutiny when they eventually discovered that their voyage would be longer and more dangerous than a straightforward trading mission to the Mediterranean.

Still deeply suspicious, Burleigh decided to spy on

Drake by means of Doughty. He summoned Doughty for several interviews, and soon found out that Drake's real intention was to sail to Panama and beyond. This was Doughty's first act of treachery towards his friend; there would be more in the next two years. Drake heard a few whispers of Doughty's business with Burleigh, and asked him bluntly what it had all been about. Doughty assured Drake that he had simply been offered a post as Burleigh's private secretary, and Drake accepted the tale happily.

Burleigh saw that it was far too late to have the expedition called off; and then international politics overtook him. Senor de Guaras was found to have been corresponding, illegally, with Mary Queen of Scots. He was imprisoned in the Tower of London. The English people were hot for open war with Spain.

Drake used some of the initial investment money to build a new ship, the *Pelican*. The builders did a fine job; though she was quite small, only 80 feet from stem to stern, she was thoroughly seaworthy, swift and easy to manoeuvre. He also had her hull covered with an additional layer of wood to protect her from the worst effects of rot and the marine worms that would gnaw their way into the wood of all ships at sea for long periods.

As the days grew colder and darker, and the time for departure came close, both Drake and Doughty brooded on the journey ahead. They had both calculated that it would only last a year, but there were too many uncertainties ahead for either of them to feel confident. The Straits of Magellan were so notoriously dangerous that the Spanish had long since given up the attempt to reach the Pacific by sea, and had instead crossed from ocean to ocean by land, in Panama. And then there were the Spanish warships, and who knew what other hazards? Early in September, Doughty drew up and signed a will, in case he should never return.

He never returned.

Chapter Seven

Circumnavigation: Setting Sail

At five o'clock on the afternoon of 15 November 1577, the skies already dark and the rain falling, Drake set sail from Plymouth. Almost at once, a sudden storm blew them back to Falmouth, and then to Plymouth again for repairs. After this inauspicious false start, they navigated their way out to sea. Drake's flagship was the *Pelican* – soon, a few months into their mission, to be re-christened with the name by which posterity remembers it: the *Golden Hind*. It weighed a hundred tons, and carried eighteen big guns, each one capable of firing a nine-pound shot, as well as a formidable arsenal of smaller weapons. It was, in short, a compact but powerful pirate ship.

The other four ships, smaller, were:

The *Elizabeth* – eighty tons and sixteen guns, captained by John Winter, who was Drake's second-in-command for the voyage;

The *Marygold* – thirty tons and sixteen guns, captained

by John Thomas;

The *Swan* – a victualling ship of fifteen tons (John Chester);

And the *Christopher* (Thomas Moone).

On board these ships were four small pinnaces, stowed away below deck in sections, ready for re-assembly when they were needed.

In all, the five crews added up to a total of 164 men and boys, including an apothecary, a shoemaker, a smith, a preacher (Francis Fletcher, who left a lively account of his experiences), soldiers trained for land actions, and ten gentleman adventurers, including Thomas Doughty and his brother John. They had food, water and alcoholic drinks enough for eighteen months, though they planned to stock up with fresh goods wherever they could steal or buy them,

Drake, fond of show to the point of ostentation, intended to live in style on this epic journey. The Queen had given him the parting gift of an embroidered sea-cap, joined to a green scarf with red bands, on which gold letters spelled out the phrase "The Lord guide and preserve thee until the end." He also had his self-appointed coat of arms, a globe and a star, engraved on the ship's bronze cannon.

Drake was as fond of sweet music as he was of good food, and brought with him string players and trumpeters, to accompany him when he dined. The furniture of his cabin was made of fine oak, and all the vessels on his table were silver, and also bore his arms. At table, he was attended behind his chair by a page – another family member, his fourteen-year-old cousin John Drake, who, in the course of the next few years, became something of a surrogate son to the childless captain. At nights, the two Drakes would often pass their time in making drawings and paintings: a form of relaxation, but also, when they were in sight of coasts, an important visual record for future English mariners.

But Drake's most valued possessions were the tools of his trade as a mariner. He had a map of the world, bought in Lisbon – the best of its kind, but, as he was to find in the Pacific, still woefully inaccurate in places. He also owned three valuable books of navigation, as well as compasses, needles, and astrolabes. Every time they took a new prize, Drake's first concern was to plunder every new navigational aid he could find.

According to some sources, the voyage began under a cloud of ill rumour. Drake had been quietly told that his friend Doughty – one of the few who knew of the real purpose of their mission -- had been boasting about his own importance and slighting Drake. Doughty claimed that it was he who had won Drake his command, and that his authority was at least equal to Drake's, if not superior. He spoke in cryptic but menacing terms about mutiny and murder. Drake recklessly refused to listen to this gossip, and carried on treating Doughty as if they were the best of friends.

Only when they caught sight of the coast of Africa, in mid-December, did Drake let the ships' companies know the true story. Their destination was not Alexandria but Morocco, then Brazil, then the Straits of Magellan and beyond. One of the mariners complained to Winter that "Mr Drake hired him for Alexandria…. He would have been hanged in England rather than have come on this voyage." But most of the men took the announcement calmly. Their only real resentment – and it would deepen as the journey continued – was against the Gentlemen. Out at sea, class distinction was at best a nuisance, at worst a danger. Every soul had to pull his weight. But the Gentlemen refused to do any of the real work, and simply lounged around in idleness while the rough sailors clambered around in the rigging. The sailors grew more and more angry and disgusted.

On the way, the fleet indulged in some minor acts of piracy, and then one major coup. They captured a large Spanish vessel of forty tons, taken her crew prisoner, and then added their prize to the fleet, giving the stolen ship the name *Christopher*, in honour of Christopher Hatton.

They sailed on to the Cape Verde islands, controlled by Portugal, where they now took a Portuguese passenger ship, the *Santa Maria*, which they renamed the *Mary*. As a show of confidence in his friend, Drake made Doughty its captain, and sent his twenty-two year old brother, Thomas Drake, to serve under Doughty. The *Mary* was a fine ship, with an excellent stock of wine, but the most valuable part of the new prize was not treasure but a man: Nuno da Silva – an experienced pilot who knew the Brazilian coast well.

Da Silva was a small, dark-skinned man of about sixty, who sported a long beard that gave him the air of a prophet. The pilot was to prove a great asset to Drake's expedition; he has also been a great asset to historians, since his reports on the next fifteen months of the three-year voyage are among the most detailed, sharp-eyed and disinterested accounts that have come down to us. Da Silva was surprisingly free of resentment about the exploit as a whole, but he did make clear that he joined Drake only after threats of violence.

Their final port of call before the Atlantic crossing was the island of La Brava. Here, Drake put ashore all the Portuguese prisoners, and ordered the *Mary* to be re-fitted as a supply ship. Then Drake heard some worrying news. His trumpeter, Brewer, told Drake that he had evidence that Doughty had been pilfering some valuables from the *Mary's* cargo – in complete violation of the code that captured property belonged to the whole company. Drake went over to the *Mary* and confronted his friend.

Doughty's response was a blustering denial, followed by the claim that it was not he but Thomas Drake who had been pilfering. Drake had Doughty's cabin searched, and found a few small valuables – a ring, some coins. Doughty claimed that these had been tokens of esteem, given to him by the Portuguese in gratitude for their clement treatment. It may have been true. Even so, Drake was enraged that Doughty had tried to incriminate young Thomas, and he shouted at him that this amounted to an act of conspiracy against his General. He sent Doughty back in disgrace to the *Pelican*; but the argument was soon patched up by one of Doughty's friends, and Drake trusted Doughty again. Or, at least, pretended to trust him.

Just before the fleet set sail, Drake supplied his Portuguese captives with one of the pinnaces he had brought in pieces from England, gave them plenty of food and water, and wished them a safe and pleasant journey back to Santiago. It was one of Drake's most gracious acts of generosity in victory. For the start of the Atlantic crossing, Drake remained on the *Mary*; he allowed Doughty to stay on the *Pelican*, in charge of the body of soldiers who would be needed on the other side of the ocean, but who were, for the time being, not much more than idle passengers.

It was now that Doughty's treachery came into the open. Once they were well out at sea, he began to bribe and flatter the master of the *Pelican*, Thomas Cuttill. Doughty had, he said, "a good liking for him", and he offered Cuttill one hundred pounds if he would take his side against Drake in any mutinous action, adding that Burleigh and his other friends at Court would look favourably on him. The temptation appears to have worked. At any rate, Cuttill did not do his obvious duty, which would have been to inform Drake at once of any seditious activity or talk. The Chaplain, Fletcher, also suspected that something dangerous was in the offing, but, again, Doughty managed to persuade him to keep silent.

Meanwhile, the small fleet had run into trouble with the weather. On some days they were hurled around by violent winds; on others they languished without any wind at all, and baked under the sun. Drake had never known anything like these dangerous and frustrating obstacles. Like his men and his monarch, he believed in demons and evil spirits, and wondered if some malevolent sorcerer had put a curse on him and his enterprise. As he and his brother lay out on the decks of the *Mary* at night, too hot to sleep, he mused on the rumours of Doughty's malicious intent, and on the possibility that his former friend was the evil sorcerer.

Matters came to a head when Drake sent his trumpeter Brewer over to the *Pelican* on an errand. Under Doughty's leadership, Brewer was treated to some rough and none too amiable horseplay. He rowed back to the *Mary* and gave his report. Drake fell into another of his noisy rages, and commanded Doughty to be brought over. When the boat drew up alongside the *Mary*, Drake shouted down that Doughty should not, after all, be let on board, but taken over to the *Swan*, to be held as a prisoner by her captain, John Sarocold "as one suspected for a conjurer".

On 5 April 1578, fifty-four days after sailing from Cape Verde, the fleet sighted land. As Nuno da Silva recalled it, they first stopped to collect fresh water from the mouth of the Rio de la Plata, but it is almost certain that they made the coast somewhere north of there. It was an ill-omened arrival. Drake, already deeply concerned about the supernatural enemies ranged against him, was still more deeply alarmed when he saw the natives chanting incantations – spells, he assumed, to bring bad weather again. He felt his fears confirmed when, as he expected, a terrifying thunderstorm blew up and made the day as black as night.

When the rain finally stopped and the skies cleared, Drake saw that the *Christopher* had disappeared. He searched for it anxiously for three days; found it; then brought it back to their mooring only to find that the *Swan* had also gone missing. Their bad luck was starting to defy belief: another great storm rained down on them, at the end of which the *Mary* had disappeared. Drake was more certain than ever of who was guilty for this series of blows, and he shouted aloud that Doughty was a witch and a conjurer and the master spirit behind the frightening weather. He soon found fervent corroboration among his crew, who said that John Doughty and his brother Thomas had boasted that they "could conjure as well as any men, and could raise the devil, and make him to meet any man in the likeness of a bear, a lion, or a man in harness."

Meanwhile, there were other, less dramatic obstacles

to the expedition's progress. They needed fresh water, and food, and their ships urgently needed to be careened and repaired after the Atlantic crossing. They had not been able to find suitable places to drop anchor, so they edged southwards along the coast until the spotted a likely bay, where they harboured. It was here that, when they went ashore in search of food, one of the most bizarre episodes of the circumnavigation took place. Or so one source relates.

Among those who joined in these modest explorations was the chaplain, Fletcher, whose narrative assures us that all the country to the south of the River Plate was inhabited by giants. Friendly giants, at that, who would make peaceable overtures to the Englishmen and join in their meals. One of them, curious to taste wine for the first time, was made instantly drunk, and fell over in such a deep slumber that everyone assumed he was dead. He soon sobered up, though, and indicated that he had enjoyed the experience so much that he wanted more!

Fletcher, a sort of budding anthropologist – or perhaps simply a chronic teller of tall tales – gave an account of Giant Society. They had mastered fire, he said, creating it by rubbing sticks of wood together; their chief joys were music and dancing; and they were extraordinarily kind – kinder, Fletcher says, than his fellow priests had been to him back in England. (Perhaps this was less a fantasy than a veiled satire on English churchmen?)

Another of Fletcher's tall tales was the behaviour of the local sea birds, which would come and perch on the heads and shoulders of the Englishmen in such great numbers that they were in danger of being dragged down to the ground and suffocated. Fletcher's yarns about the ostriches, which, he said, marched in rank and file to the commands of their ostrich-captains, are probably best left in the archives.

Curiously, large parts of Fletcher's account have some basis in reality. There were no giants in the region, not any military ostriches, but there were Indians, who at first regarded the Englishmen with suspicion, and then grew more and more friendly. Drake had learned the wisdom of forming alliances with local peoples, and he ordered that various presents be left close to the shore. The locals came out to investigate, decided that these strangers were benevolent, and were soon won over. They invited the sailors to join in the dances – to the delight of his men, Winter joined in with gusto – and both sides enjoyed the novelty. The Indians' friendliness did not inhibit them from stealing anything on which they could lay their hands, but Drake ordered his men to tolerate these small thefts cheerfully.

It was now that Drake made the drastic decision that the *Swan* should be broken up, and her crew transferred to the *Pelican*. Drake summoned her captain, John Sarocold, to report on Doughty's conduct over the previous weeks. Sarocold's account was damning. Though Doughty had notionally been a prisoner, he had enjoyed more than enough liberty to begin stirring up mutiny again. Doughty had taken aside the captain of soldiers, John Chester, and urged him to strip Sarocold of his command by force. He also insisted that his authority was at least equal to Drake's if not superior, and that he knew many dark secrets about Drake's private life which rendered him unfit to be their leader. But Chester had not been swayed.

While the *Swan* was being broken up, Drake interviewed Doughty about these allegations. At first the former friends spoke calmly enough, but the tone grew more heated, up to the point when Doughty bragged that "the lightest word that came out of his mouth was to be believed as soon as the General's oath." That was enough. Drake punched him, and ordered that he be strapped to the mast to suffer in the harsh sunlight. At nightfall, he ordered that both Doughty and his brother John be held prisoner again on the *Christopher*, to await trial for mutiny. This was done, and almost immediately yet another storm broke out, and once again the *Christopher* was blown far out of sight. Even the least superstitious of men might have seen this as confirmation that the Doughty brothers were indeed warlocks.

It took another three days of searching before the *Christopher* was found. Drake decided that this ship should also be broken up. Then he was rowed over to the *Elizabeth*, where he told the captain that Thomas Doughty was "a conjurer and a seditious fellow", and that John Doughty was "a witch and a poisoner". The brothers, he ordered, must not be addressed by any crew member; neither must they be allowed to read or write. The latter might seem a little excessive, until we understand it from Drake's perspective. The reading and writing he had forbidden was the reading and writing of spells. There was no doubt at all in his mind now that the Doughty brothers were agents of Satan.

They had many challenges ahead of them, but before the expedition could proceed, the brothers must be tried.

Chapter Eight

Circumnavigation: The Trial and Death of Doughty

By 19 June 1578, their long series of misfortunes finally seemed at an end. A few miles from the next destination, Port San Julian, they finally caught sight of the *Mary*, which almost everyone had assumed to be sunk in the dreadful storm. The small reunited fleet of four ships – *Pelican, Elizabeth, Marygold, Mary* – sailed slowly towards the bay. Located at 49 degrees, the Port was further south than any English vessels had ever ventured before. This would be their last major stop before attempting the Magellan Straits.

The following day, 20 June, they dropped anchor. Two days later, a lightly armed landing party of six men, plus Drake as leader, went ashore – with terrible consequences. So far, their treatment by the Indians had been so consistently friendly that they were quite calm when a group of natives came out to greet them in a friendly manner. This amicable mood was shattered when Robert Winter, showing off to the Indians how an English bow worked, broke his bow-string. One of them, convinced that the English were now disarmed, shot an arrow into Winter's chest and killed him. A sailor named Oliver, who had the only gun – more exactly, an "arquebus", an early version of what later became the musket and then the rifle – tried to shoot Winter's killer, but the weapon misfired, and Oliver himself was killed with an arrow.

The five survivors ran a short distance away, then turned to face the Indians who were coming for them, still shooting arrows. Drake ordered the men with shields to form a wall behind which the rest could take shelter. Then he grabbed Oliver's arquebus, reloaded it, and blasted it at short range into the Indian who had first shed blood. His body was blown apart, and the Indians retreated. They never returned.

Exploring the mainland in greater detail, they found a "spruce mast". Most of the men assumed that this must be the remains of the gibbet from which Magellan had hanged his miscreant crewmen fifty-eight years earlier. They were right: a brief investigative dig around its base soon yielded human bones. The cooper of the *Pelican* was inspired to cut chunks of wood from the gibbet, and to make tankards from them.

In case the Indians should ever decide to attack them again, Drake ordered the men to pitch their tents on a small island in the bay. It was time for Doughty to be brought to trial, and it was on this small island that it now took place.

Drake gathered the entire company together on 30 June. For some reason, he decided not to bring charges against the younger brother. Nor did he make mention –

though there is little doubt that he was certain it was true – that either brother had been using black magic. According to Cooke, who was no great admirer of the General, Drake's indictment ran:

> "Thomas Doughty, you have sought by divers means, inasmuch as you may, to discredit me to the great hindrance and overthrow of this voyage, besides other great matters which I have to charge you, the which, if you can clear yourself withal, you and I shall be very good friends, whereto the contrary, you have deserved death."

Doughty denied these charges, though he offered nothing in the way of concrete alibis. At this point, Drake might have been expected to bring forward his witnesses, have their statements heard, and then pronounce a death sentence. Instead, he asked Doughty how he would like to be tried. Doughty replied that he wished to be taken back to England and tried there. It was an impossible request. So Drake chose forty men to make up a formal jury – impartially, it seems, since at least three of the jurors were allies of Doughty.

Drake finally brought forward his witnesses, one of whom was Edward Bright, who pronounced under oath that he had heard Doughty's seditious talk while they were still at Plymouth. Doughty interrupted by blurting out that Burleigh, who was meant to be kept in the dark about the true ambition of Drake's voyage, had known it all along. Drake indignantly denied that this could be possible. Doughty, equally impassioned, said that he knew quite well that Burleigh was in on the secret, because "He had it from me." In a single phrase, Doughty had admitted to having betrayed Drake before they had even left England.

There were more witnesses: Cutill, Sarocold, and others, but by now their testimonies were pretty much superfluous. Doughty's friend Mr. Vicary, who was a lawyer, objected to the proceedings and said that the jury was not legally competent to pass a death sentence. Drake replied, with some anger, that they were not being asked any such thing. Their sole job was to decide whether Doughty were innocent or guilty. Drake himself would determine the penalty.

According to Nuno da Silva, Drake now produced a sheaf of papers, kissed them, and read them out loud. "All present saw the papers were his and from her [i.e. Elizabeth], and that it was by her authority that he was executing Doughty." But he still consulted the jury for one last time. He asked them for a show of hands to decide whether Doughty should be executed.

The verdict was unanimous, or as near as made no difference. Doughty must die. Drake said that the sentence would be carried out on the day after next, on 2 July, adding that if anyone could think of a reason why Doughty might be spared with no potential danger for the rest of the voyage, he would listen to them carefully. But no such reasons were produced.

What happened next reads strangely to modern eyes, and reminds us again how differently men thought and acted in an age of faith. Doughty, seeing that he was far beyond reprieve, decided to meet his end with grace, gaiety and calm. He asked to receive Communion for the last time, and asked Drake to join him. This they did, kneeling together humbly at a makeshift altar. Then they sat together to have a hearty dinner as if they were once again the best of friends, talked cheerfully and drank to each others' health.

They drew aside for a short private conversation, and then Doughty was led in procession to the block. Doughty knelt, and prayed for his Queen and for the success of Drake's expedition, and finally begged Drake to forgive any of the other crew members whom he might be under suspicion as mutineers. Drake gave his word. Doughty laid his head on the block, and the axe fell. His severed head was held up for the men and boys to gaze on.

"Lo!", Drake shouted. "This is the end of traitors."

Drake's fleet remained in St Julian throughout July – the heart of winter in the southern hemisphere. Drake knew that, after the execution of Doughty, he must do his best to ride out any lingering resentment among the man's allies, and to re-unite the company in a single purpose. Then, on 11 August he ordered the entire company to make their Confessions to the Chaplain, and to take the Sacrament.

This done, he summoned everyone ashore and gave a long and spirited speech – part sermon, part offering of terms, part pep-talk. Making no mention of the recent execution, he said that he had seen a mutinous spirit developing because of the working sailors' anger with the idleness and arrogance of the Gentlemen. *"By the life of God, it doth even take my wits from me to think on it."* Then came his punch-line. *"The gentleman in the future must haul and draw with the mariner, and the mariner with the gentleman."*

Before the import of this had fully sunk in, Drake said something even more unexpected. He addressed the ships' officers, and told that from now on and until the end of the voyage, they were demoted to the rank of ordinary seamen. There were angry shouts from the officers, but Drake faced them down, and reminded them that the Queen had given him ultimate authority.

He then said that if enough of the company dissented strongly from his new policy, he would give them the *Marygold* to sail back to England. They should be wary, though: *"... for if I find them in my way, I will surely sink them."* Not a single mariner raised his hand to accept the offer.

Seeing he had won the day, Drake now decided to be more moderate. He at once restored all the officers to their former ranks, and he declared that there would be no further investigation into the plots fomented by Doughty. The slate was wiped clean. It was a simple, bold performance, and it worked perfectly. For the rest of the voyage, the men were firmly united in their struggle against the enemy and the elements.

As the final part of their preparations, Drake ordered the *Mary* burned; he wanted the men to be divided between just three ships, to minimise the danger of their being separated by the storms ahead. The fleet weighed anchor on 17 August 1578. Three days later, it reached the opening of the Straits of Magellan.

Chapter Nine

Circumnavigation:
The *Golden Hind* in the Pacific

By now, Drake's Portuguese prize the *Mary* was so leaky and unseaworthy that he decided to cut his losses and break her up. Now he had just three ships, the *Elizabeth*, the *Marygold* and the *Pelican*, which he decided to rechristen as the *Golden Hind* – a tribute to his patron Sir Christopher Hatton, who had a hind for his crest. They sailed on until 20 August, when they rounded the Cape and entered the hazardous sea-corridor that led to the Pacific. As they passed by the cliffs of the mainland, Drake ordered that all three vessels should strike their topsails in honour of Queen Elizabeth.

Their passage was difficult. The winds were against them, and they often went astray into land-locked inlets or almost came aground. Their charts were unreliable. Drake himself would often sail ahead to test out the way in a small boat. It began to feel as if they were entering a different, demonic world. On shore, they could see the lights and smoke from native fires, though not the natives themselves. They were also visited by "fowls that could not fly, of the bigness of geese" – in fact penguins, who approached them unafraid and were duly slaughtered by the hundred. Penguin flesh was found to be tasty and wholesome, and those birds which were not eaten at once were gutted and salted for future use.

Fighting the cold winds, they sailed west, then south, then west again… and then, on 6 September 1578, they finally reached the Pacific. Five years after Drake's vision of sailing on an English vessel into the Southern Sea, he had realized his ambition. Almost immediately, the weather look set to dash the triumph from his hand.

On 7 September, a terrible storm came in from the north. The ships were driven southwards, far into unknown waters. It blew for a full two weeks, and one night the terrors of riding it out were deepened by a lunar eclipse. Had they offended God by venturing where they were not meant to go? When the winds finally eased, the *Marygold* was nowhere to be seen. The *Elizabeth* and the *Golden Hind* sought refuge near the mouth of the Strait, but once again a huge storm blew up. Drake decided to attempt to escape out to the open sea, and the two ships lost sight of each other.

For three weeks, Mr Winter, captain of the *Elizabeth*, waited to see if the *Golden Hind* would return. With great reluctance, he concluded that she must have been lost at sea. Instead of following the agreed plan of sailing northwards up the coast to a pre-arranged rendezvous point, he despaired of the whole enterprise, and sailed eastwards back through the Strait and from there set course for England. On arrival, he narrated his version of the events to the historian Stow, emphasising the soundness of his decision and casting Drake in the blackest of terms. This was a safety measure: Winter was well aware that, if Drake had somehow survived, and in the course of time also returned to England, he might be at risk of trial for desertion.

In fact, the *Golden Hind* had survived with relatively slight damage, and Drake had no intention of heading home for quite a while – not least because his accidental journey far south had brought him a major revelation. Among the documents Drake had brought with him was his copy of Magellan's *Discovery*, in the English translation by Richard Eden, first published in 1555. Magellan had advanced the widely accepted theory – the same in which Dee and his colleagues believed – that the South American continent continued to stretch southwards into Polar regions, and became a *Terra Australis* that ran downwards into the ice fields.

But the storm had driven the *Golden Hind* far south, and Drake saw no land; only ocean. He concluded that the "Atlantic and South Sea meet in a most large and free scope." There was no such thing as a *Terra Australis*. Purely by accident, he had made one of the greatest geographical discoveries ever.

There were, however, some small islands in these otherwise open waters, and Drake, claiming them in the name of Her Majesty, called them the "Elizabethides", or Elizabeth Island. As the ship's chaplain, Fletcher, later recalled: "Seeking out the most southernmost [sic] part of the island, [Drake] cast himself down on the uttermost point grovelling, and reached out his body over it." Together, they put up a stone on which they carved the name of the Queen and the date. At least in principle, England now owned some territory in the Pacific.

Having staked his patriotic claim, Drake returned to the urgent business at hand. He had made an arrangement with his two other captains that, in the event they should be separated, they would aim for a rendezvous on the coast of Chile. On 30 October he set sail northwards, using Spanish maps as his guide. According to these charts, the Chilean coast ran sharply to the north-west, and yet day after day went by, and there was still no sight of land. His chaplain, Fletcher, suggested that it was possible that these maps were deliberately wrong, and designed by the Spanish cartographers to mislead any enemy mariners who might use them. This seemed a plausible idea, so Drake altered his course to the east.

Their first landfall was on an island known to the Spanish as Mucho. The crew took on fresh water, but as they did so they were set upon by the inhabitants. Several were severely injured, and Drake himself took wounds in his face and the top of his head. There was no surgeon to treat them – one of them had died, the other was on the *Elizabeth* – and the care of the wounded fell to a young boy "whose goodwill was more remarkable than any skill he had." Despite this, they all made decent recoveries. Reflecting on the incident, Drake grew more and more convinced that the locals had mistaken them for Spaniards. If he was right, and he could trust in the principle that "my enemy's enemy is my friend", their chances of finding allies in the months ahead were looking good. He ordered his crew that there must be no reprisals.

They reached the Chilean coast, but found no sign of the other ships. No matter: Drake's blood was up. He set sail still further northwards, in search of potential new allies among the natives and signs of his old enemy, the Spanish. The former soon appeared in the form of a friendly Indian who they found peacefully fishing. He was taken on board the *Golden Hind*, where he exchanged courtesies in sign language and rudimentary Spanish. Their guest told them about the prosperous city of Valparaiso, further up the coast, where they could take on food and water… and perhaps some prizes, too. Following his directions, they arrived in the harbour of Valparaiso on 5 December.

Almost immediately, the English carried out an audacious raid. It was almost comically easy for them. Ahead of them, at anchor, was a large Spanish ship, freighted with valuables: gold worth some £8,000, 1770 jars of wine, and all manner of minor treasures. There were just eight Spanish sailors on board, and when they saw the modest *Golden Hind* draw up, they assumed that it must be one of their own country's vessels. They drummed a welcome, and cheerily invited the newcomers on board to drink a few bottles of wine. Drake despatched Thomas Moone and few other men to take up the kind invitation; as soon as they were on board, Moone lashed around him with his sword, shouting "Go down, Dog!"

One of the Spanish sailors jumped overboard and swam to freedom; the other seven were made captive and sent ashore. The *Golden Hind* sailed out back out to sea, accompanied by its rich new prize. And the Spanish now knew for a certainty that Drake, the old monster, was in the Pacific.

For about another month, Drake sailed along the coast, hoping to meet up with his two missing ships. At the end of the year he decided that the task was fruitless, and turned his ships northwards for a piratical spree.

Some of his raids did not even require a shot to be fired. At a coastal town named Tarapaca they saw a Spaniard fast asleep on a sunny beach, with four thousand ducats' worth of silver piled up by his side. (How this had come about was anyone's guess.) Drake sent a small team ashore, and they removed the silver so quietly that the man did not even stir in his sleep.

There were a few minor scuffles with fishing boats, some successful, some thwarted by the cunning of the fishermen. Then there was a foiled attempt to hunt down and capture a major Spanish ship of which they had heard rumour when they put in at Arica. At first, the chase seemed successful; but when Drake boarded this vessel, he discovered that they crew had been warned of his imminent attack, and had abandoned ship, taking all the treasure with them. As a minor act of vengeance, Drake had his crew set the empty ship's sails, and then send it out westwards, never to be seen again.

Drake's next major exploit was his raid on the port of Callao de Lima – one of the principal ports of departure for the treasure ships bound for Panama. Uncertain how heavily the place was defended with big guns, he made his way quietly into port just after sundown on 15 February 1579. Five Spanish ships were at anchor there, and nobody raised an alarm. Either everyone was asleep, or, once again, the men on watch had taken the *Golden Hind* to be a Spanish ship. He sent out a small craft to make stealthy acts of burglary, but the pickings were slender – a single case of bullion and some silks.

While these minor raids were in progress, another Spanish ship, from Panama, sailed into harbour and came to anchor close to the *Golden Hind* – again, not suspecting that she was an English ship. But by now, the watchmen on shore were starting to have their doubts, and they sent out a small boast to investigate. Challenged to identify himself, Drake whispered to his Spanish prisoner to shout out that he was a Chilean vessel, under the command of Captain Miguel Angelo, a well-known ally of the Spanish.

It was a good try, but it backfired. One of the men on the small boat was an old friend of the real Miguel Angelo, so he clambered up the side of the *Golden Hind* to greet his pal. Instead of a familiar face, he saw a gun – a huge gun of the kind no trading ship would ever carry. He slid back down, rowed back ashore, and raised the alarm. It was time to run. Drake's first move was to hamper his enemy before the enemy could prepare for a fight – he had his men cut the cables and masts of all five ships at anchor around him. The maimed ships drifted, bumped into each other, grew hopelessly entangled, and were rendered incapable of pursuit for many hours.

The only Spanish vessel to escape this treatment was the newly arrived ship from Panama, which made a bid for freedom. The bid was short-lived. Drake promptly seized her, sent two men to grab as much loot as they could in a brief session, and then set full sail out to sea. More valuable than any of the minor booty that his sailors had managed to steal was a juicy piece of information: just two weeks earlier, a large Spanish vessel, *"Our Lady of the Conception"*, had set sail for Panama freighted with gold. It was exactly the kind of treasure for which Drake craved, and he wanted to overtake and capture the *"Conception"* before it reached its destination.

Once again, though, the winds were against him – or, more exactly, they simply dropped for two days, leaving the *Golden Hind* languishing not very far from port. Meanwhile, the Viceroy of Peru, who had just heard of Drake's raid, despatched soldiers to Callao so that they could be boarded on ships and sent off to attack the English thief. But the wind still failed to rise, and if Drake could not yet escape, his enemies could not yet pursue. Stalemate.

Finally, the wind started to blow fitfully, and then strongly, and it whisked the light, highly manoeuvrable *Golden Hind* far away from the pursuing ships. Within a day, they had not only left the Spanish forces well behind them, but capped their escape by taking a frigate. They sailed close to shore, in the hope that they might gather news of the *"Conception"*, which would have needed to pause from time to time for water and provisions. Soon, they learned that their quarry was not far ahead. First, just off the coast of Paita, they boarded a ship whose sailors told them that the *"Conception"* had put into shore there just two days earlier.

Next, they overtook a Spanish ship bound for Panama. Her captain told Drake that the *"Conception"* had passed his ship by on the previous day. With a strong wind behind Drake was closing in. He offered a chain of gold to the first man to sight her. He knew that there might be a bloody fight ahead of them, since the *"Conception"* was so heavily equipped with artillery that it had earned the nickname *Cacafuego* – a name that genteel historians used to translate as "Spitfire", but in fact means "Shitfire".

At three in the afternoon of 1 March 1579, the Admiral's page, John Drake, shouted down from his perch on the mast of *Golden Hind* that he had spotted the *Cacafuego* about three miles ahead of them; and he bragged that the golden chain was his.

Drake's next move has divided historians. He gave the order that a number of used wine casks, now charged with water, should be thrown over the stern on ropes. Why? Nuno da Silva thought that it was because the *Golden Hind* was riding stern-heavy in the waves, and that this weight behind her would elevate to bow and speed their advance. Others believed quite the opposite: Drake did not want to attack until nightfall, and he did not wish to make it obvious that the *Cacafuego* was being pursued, so he had put on the brakes.

If this was his plan, it worked even more effectively than he may have hoped. Like other captains before him, the captain of the *Cacafuego*, Juan de Anton, mistook the *Golden Hind* for a friendly ship, put his own vessel about to greet his fellow countrymen, and drew up alongside. Drake shouted at him, ordering de Anton to strike sail and surrender. The Spanish captain refused, so Drake's men opened fire with arrows and guns. The *Cacafuego*'s mizzen was shot overboard, and armed crewmen from the *Golden Hind* stormed the decks. The Spanish made no effort to resist them, and fled below deck. Captain de Anton was made prisoner, and the *Cacafuego* was taken without an injury on either side.

The two ships then put out to sea, sailing for two nights and a day, until Drake thought they were safe enough to pause and take stock of their plunder. It was immense. Working hard, it took four days to transfer treasure from the *Cacafuego* to the *Golden Hind* – twenty-six tons of silver in bars, thirteen chests of silver coins, eighty pounds of gold, piles of jewels and fine pearls… The pilot's boy said that the *Shitfire* should now be renamed the *Shitsilver*, *"which pretty speech of the pilot's boy ministered matter for laughter to us both then and long after."*

As was his way, Drake treated his captive with a generosity and frankness that, from our perspective, seems almost beyond belief. He entertained Juan de Anton as an honoured guest, dined lavishly with him – Drake's Spanish was not too bad, though it was an effort for him to speak it at any length – showed him all over the *Golden Hind* and even discussed with reckless honesty his plans for the immediate future. Once his men had hauled all the treasure on board, Drake signed a formal and accurate receipt and solemnly handed it over. Finally, he gave de Anton a letter of safe conduct that would ensure his safety should he ever be taken prisoner by other English ships – and particularly if he should be taken by the *Elizabeth* and its captain John Winter. It began:

> "Master Winter, if it pleaseth God you
> should chance to meet with this ship of
> Senor Juan de Anton, I pray you should use
> him well according to my word and promise
> given them: and if you want anything that is
> in this ship of Senor Juan de Anton, I pray
> you pay them double the value of it, which
> I will satisfy again: and command your men
> not to do her any hurt...."

He ended with the words:

> "Your Sorrowful Captain, whose heart is
> heavy for you,
> FRANCIS DRAKE"

As the *Cacafuego* sailed away, Drake stood on deck and gave Senor de Anton a cheerful salute. That night he dined formally with young John Drake standing behind his chair in waiting, and sporting his new chain. When they had finished their meal, Drake dismissed his musicians for the night, and settled down with John to their favourite pastime on quiet occasions – making drawings.

What next? Now that he had plundered the *Cacafuego*, the Spanish navy would soon be out in search of him. He had originally planned to make a direct raid on Panama, but now that the city was on alert, it was far too dangerous for him. Besides, the *Golden Hind* was now so stuffed with silver and gold that there was simply no more room to store much additional plunder. It was two months since he had lost contact with the *Elizabeth* and the *Marygold*, and he had, sensibly, given up hope of finding them in these waters. Time to flee before they were caught, and then to set a course for home.

There were three possible routes: south, west or north. Drake knew that by this time the route south – via the Straits of Magellan – would be blocked by Spanish ships from Chile and Peru. Though he did not yet know that the *Elizabeth* had made it through just in time, he was quite aware that, for the *Golden Hind*, the southward route would mean almost certain capture, and worse. So it would not be South.

North? That route had never been sailed, but in theory it was a possibility. It would mean a trip into Arctic waters, and a navigation of the legendary North-West passage from the west. One of the other great Elizabethan mariners, Martin Frobisher, was attempting it from the east. Drake had an old map of the North-West Passage, dating from the fourteenth century, but he did not know how reliable it might be. He showed it to Nuno da Silva, who recalled that Drake pointed out "a strait situated at 66 degrees N., saying that he had to go there, and that if he did not find an opening, he would have to go back to China."

West? That would mean crossing the Pacific, then rounding the Cape of Good Hope and then sailing northwards past Africa and so back to England. All things considered, this was probably the least hazardous, and it would give Drake the prestige of being the first Englishman to sail round the world. Since it was Drake's temperament to seek rather than flee hazard whenever he thought he had a fighting chance, he put the westward option to the back of his mind, and prepared for the voyage north, which would be a good deal shorter. His crew were with him, even though they knew the risks – not least of which was the possibility of losing all the riches they had recently won.

Drake duly set sail for the coast of Nicaragua, where he planned to take on water and food. Their voyage soon proved lively. First, he captured a Spanish frigate – it was loaded with a product unknown to Englishmen, sarsaparilla – and brought it into bay. Here, much of the treasure from the *Cacafuego* was transferred to the frigate, under armed guard, so that the *Golden Hind* could be careened, cleansed and given a thorough overhaul.

While his own ship was being repaired, Drake took his new ship out on a scouting trip, and promptly captured another frigate. Among its crew were some Chinese pilots; even though Drake was still set on the northerly course, he saw how useful these men and their charts would be should he eventually change his mind and decide that the North-West route was, after all, the wrong choice. Drake ordered all the sarsaparilla dumped in the sea, and in the last week of March set off again, with the plan of making their next stop at Guatulco (or Huatulco as it is now known on the Mexican coast).

Little more than a week later, on 4 April 1579, he captured yet another Spanish frigate in a dawn action. Her captain was one Don Francisco Zarate, and we know what happened when Drake boarded because Don Francisco wrote a detailed letter about it to Drake's old enemy, Don Martino Enriquez.

The Spanish gave up without any attempt at resistance. Zarate was brought on board the *Golden Hind* where he met Drake, whom he described as being a short man of about 35, with a fair beard. Drake interrogated him quite fiercely, and asked whether any of Enriquez's family members might be on board? But when it came time to have dinner, once again Drake treated Zarate as an honoured guest, and shared food from a single platter to reassure the Spanish captain that his food had not been poisoned. Zarate was impressed by the pomp and delicacy of the occasion: a string band played, the excellent food was served on silver plate, and Drake offered him rose water to wash his hands, commenting that it had been a present from the Queen. This may not have been entirely true.

In other respects, Zarate was not nearly so well pleased. Drake took a fancy to some of his "trifles", including a magnificent gold falcon "with a great emerald in the breast thereof." In partial recompense, Drake gave him a dagger and a silver chafing-dish. Zarate would later be sarcastic about this unequal exchange.

Despite being short-changed in this way, Zarate was highly impressed both by the captain and his company.

He would call Drake "the greatest of mariners", and, when he asked around, found that the whole crew "adored" their leader. (This contradicts the view of some historians that the tight discipline on board the *Golden Hind* was the result of fear, not love.) He was deeply impressed by the efficiency and excellent training of the sailors, and still more impressed by the ship's specialist hands – the carpenters, the caulkers and the painters of shorelines, whose work was so good that it would prove an invaluable resource to any future English ships set on exploring the western coasts of South America.

Drake liked his prisoner, but was disappointed by what he considered the paltry nature of his latest pickings: mostly Chinese porcelain and silks. He took them anyway, declaring that they would be an acceptable present for his wife Mary when he finally set up house with her in earnest.

Zarate was sent back unharmed to his ship, and Drake sailed on.

By 15 April they had reached Guatulco, the last Spanish-held port of their Pacific venture. His plans for a quiet period of watering and repairs were hampered by activities in town, where a rowdy conspiracy trial was in progress. Ever more of a warrior than a diplomat, Drake solved his logistical problem by having armed men surround the court, arrest both the accused and the jurors, and having the whole lot locked up on the *Golden Hind* while he and his men occupied the town at their leisure.

One of the temporary prisoners was the town Factor, who was greatly struck by how much time and energy was spent on the *Golden Hind* in religious observations. Drake himself, the man reported, would read prayers aloud to his officers, while the chaplain, Fletcher, took prayers with the crew. Services were held twice a day, before the mid-day meal and then before the evening meal. Surrounded by his nine officers, Drake would kneel and pray in silence for about a quarter of an hour; then he would preach a sermon; then musicians would strike up pious melodies, and the company would sing hymns and lamentations.

Finally, John Drake performed a solemn dance, which the Factor assumed to be a standard English observance, probably inspired by David dancing before the Ark. Drake told them that, even though they were Catholic, they would be permitted to join in with the singing of Psalms if they so wished. Otherwise, they could retire to their cabin on condition that they maintained complete silence.

Drake's conduct on land was very far from pious and ecumenical, and his admirers have long found his treatment of Guatulco troubling. For many years it was said that it was part of Drake's chivalry that he never allowed his men to desecrate churches. In Guatulco, though, he sent his men to pillage the local church, strip it of all its valuables, and break up all the images.

It was at this point that he also parted company with Nuno da Silva. Drake put him on board a ship bound for Panama. Da Silva later made a long and detailed deposition about his experiences as Drake's prisoner, and, as noted above, seems not to have borne any rancour towards his former captor. His account – which is one of the major sources for our knowledge of the circumnavigation – was a factual account, not a polemic.

Once more, Drake weighed up the best route home. Once more he decided that the North-West passage, being the shortest way, was the best. The *Golden Hind* sailed out of harbour, and began its way up towards the Arctic.

Chapter Ten

Circumnavigation: The Journey Home

From 16 April to 3 June 1579, the *Golden Hind* sailed a course to the north-west. Drake calculated that they were on latitude 42 degrees North, though he was far from sure that his charts were correct. As the days passed, he lost all faith in them. By his reckonings, the coast of America should be far off to their east, beyond the horizon, and yet a sudden chance of wind direction brought them back into sight of it. Where the charts showed the coastline running away to the east, their observations proved that it was in fact headed west.

The temperature began to drop, and then drop again, to the point where the riggings were frozen solid and it was impossible to keep food thawed for long enough to be chewed and swallowed. The crew were exhausted and weak from hunger, and the temperature continued to fall. Or did it? This dramatic account of hardships has baffled many historians, since no one has ever encountered such dreadfully cold weather in these climes and in the summer months. One plausible explanation is that the official account was entirely fictitious, and may be covering up a far more likely story – that the crew were so opposed to the North-West Passage policy that they were on the point of rebellion. Far better for Drake's reputation that he been seen to be thwarted by the elements than by his own men.

And even the official account of this stage of the expedition admits that morale had began to suffer, badly. It reports that the men wondered how much further into the icy waters they would have to go before Drake admitted defeat, and abandoned his quest for the North-West Passage. The answer – so the account runs – came when they reached Latitude 48 North, on a parallel with Vancouver. Drake ordered the ship to put into bay there. They did so, but alternating fogs and high winds made the stay untenable.

Drake, heeding the general pessimism, ordered the ship turned round, and the *Golden Hind* sailed southwards again until it reached latitude 38 degrees north, just north of San Francisco. The spot where they are presumed to have landed is now called "Drake's Bay" – an identification that has quite often been challenged.

Wherever they actually landed, they had urgent business. The *Golden Hind* had developed some serious leaks, which needed to be repaired as rapidly as possible. What happened next sounds like a chapter from a Rider Haggard novel, or some other rose-tinted story-book about encounters between credulous indigenous populations and white colonists.

It was a peaceful encounter, which began when local villagers sent out a man in a canoe to parlay with their strange newcomers. He could speak neither Spanish nor (of course) English, but it was clear from the way he eagerly proffered gifts of woven feathers and other ornaments that his intentions were wholly hospitable. The English offered him gifts in return; to their surprise, the only thing he would take was a hat.

Rightly confident that it was safe to set up a temporary base here, Drake and a party of builders went ashore to start constructing a palisade. At first the English were alarmed by the large numbers of men and women who gathered to watch them, and still more disconcerted by the way in which the local women would shriek wildly, and strike themselves on their heads and bare breasts, and throw themselves on the ground. Drake made an inspired guess: the locals had taken the English for gods, and were carrying out rites of propitiation.

Shocked at the impiety of this pagan notion, he ordered his men to Christian prayers, and to try to convey to the locals that this was how white men spoke to God. The locals must have been quick-witted, for it soon became clear that they had grasped what the English were doing. They gave up their own mode of worship and watched the Christian rites with close interest and increasing pleasure. They seemed particularly delighted by the singing of psalms, and made appreciative noises at this unfamiliar type of music. The next few days were far more tranquil, though there were many signs that the natives continued to regard their visitors as gods. The sailors were able to relax a little and have some much-needed rest after their ordeals on the sail north.

Finally, the locals staged a major symbolic act of diplomacy. They had summoned a *Hioh* – a tribal chief – who wore a giant crown decorated with feathers, and was attended by a formidable body-guard and a mace-bearer.

The *Hioh* gave the order for a ceremony to begin. The English watched without much comprehension beyond the basic one that this was all being done in their honour.

The mace-bearer gave a long oration about who knows what, and then there were many, many songs, and just as many dances. Then the locals signalled for Drake to sit down with the *Hioh*, and orations began again. Next, the *Hioh* performed a solemn set of actions that finally made everything clear. He took the feathered crown from his own head, and placed it on Drake's. Then he put chains of delicate, highly polished bones around Drake's neck. A huge shout went up: "*Hioh!*". They had just made Drake their new King.

Drake was none too polished as a courtier, but he saw what he must do. He made gracious gestures of pleasure and happy acceptance, and, "in the name and to the use of Her Most Excellent Majesty, took the sceptre, crown, and dignity of the said country into his hand." He was not quite King Francis, but he was Elizabeth's representative in this new land of California. He called it New Albion, and, given the uncertain state of international law at the time, he probably had every right to stake the English claim. To the best of anyone's knowledge, the only European who had been here before Drake was the Portuguese mariner Rodriquez Cabrillo, who had come ashore during an expedition of 1542. There was no evidence at all that Cabrillo had staked a claim for Portugal.

Even so, Drake's claim was more symbolic than real. Some months later, when Drake boasted to Elizabeth about her new dominion, she asked him rather sourly what was the point of having an overseas possession if you had no troops or colonists there to secure it?

According to a widely believed legend, Drake set up a brass plate to mark Elizabeth's latest land, and engraved it with the date and Her Majesty's name. He added a small box containing a portrait of Elizabeth and her heraldic achievement, plus a sixpenny piece on which he scratched his own name. This plate no longer exists, and may have been stolen, though many years later it was replaced by a replica which may or many not be accurate in its details.

It was midsummer now, and while the carpenters carried on their work on the *Golden Hind*, everyone else was free to entertain himself as he saw fit. Drake enjoyed making forays into the nearby woods, to see the exotic wildlife. He spotted huge deer, and what he thought was a "cony", or rabbit, "with the tail of a rat of great length". It seems likely that he was the first European ever to encounter a beaver, though some zoologists have suggested that the creatures may have been ground-squirrels. He noted that these big "conies" were much prized for their skins. He also saw tempting signs that the soil nearby contained deposits of gold and silver.

Others continued to relish the unfamiliar experience of being treated like gods. Partly awed, partly fascinated by these white strangers, some of the "common sort" among the natives would seek out their company, "and such as pleased their fancies (which commonly were the youngest of us), they presently, enclosing them about, offered their sacrifices to them" – which appears to mean, not that they seduced the young men but that they once again began to tear their flesh as a sign of worship. The English took pity on those who mutilated themselves, and treated them with "lotions, plasters, and ointments according to the state of their griefs." The natives were so impressed by the healing powers of these novel treatments that they brought ailing relatives along to receive similar treatments. In these exchanges, both sides grew fond of each other.

Their idyllic stay lasted a full five weeks, and at some stage of it Drake changed his mind about the North-West Passage. The *Golden Hind* would attempt to cross the Pacific. When word of their imminent departure was somehow conveyed to the locals, they fell into "sighs and sorrowings and lamentable mourning". To sooth them, the crewmen arranged Christian worship to which every-one was invited; once again, the air was filled with the sounds of prayers and chanted psalms. When the *Golden Hind* set sail, the locals built huge farewell bonfires, and stared out at sea until she disappeared over the horizon and was gone for good.

Drake set his course south-by-west, and they sailed on for two full months on open sea, until at the end of September they reached latitude 8 degrees north of the equator, and a group of inhabited islands which are today known as the Pelew Islands. A small fleet of elaborately decorated canoes rowed out to meet them, but if the English anticipated a reprise of their happy experience in New Albion, they were about to be rudely disappointed.

At first all seemed well: the Islanders seemed eager to trade food for English products. But when the goods had been handed over, the Islanders pelted the crew with stones. (Magellan had reported meeting exactly the same treat-ment, so it is surprising that Drake had not approached more warily.) The English replied with gunfire, first as warning shots above the Islanders' heads, and then directly at them. Drake ordered the anchor weighed, and the ship promptly sailed away. Angered by this event, Drake named this place the Isle of Thieves.

Two weeks later, they came within sight of the Philippines. On 3 November 1579, they reached the Spice Islands – the Moluccas. Drake had planned to make the island of Tidore – a plan that he rapidly adapted when they were greeted by a canoe, which bore an envoy from the local Sultan, Baber, whose men had spotted their approach. A few years earlier, there had been a bloody conflict with the colonising forces from Portugal. The Portuguese had, the envoy explained, killed Sultan Baber's father, chopped his body into hunks and scattered them in the sea.

The Sultan had retaliated with extreme force, and had driven the Portuguese away from his island, Ternate. For some reason, the people of Tidore had offered the Portuguese sanctuary. If Drake was not an ally of Portugal, the Sultan said, he was welcome to stay at Ternate. Drake was delighted – he hated the Portuguese almost as much as he hated the Spanish – and sent the Sultan a velvet cloak. The Sultan promptly reciprocated, and sent Drake a signet ring.

Once again, the English were treated as highly valued guests. The Sultan sent out four large canoes to sail in pomp around the *Golden Hind*. Each canoe bore a perfumed canopy, beneath which stood handsome young men from the Court. This formal greeting was soon made complete by the arrival of the Sultan himself. The crew treated him to a ceremonial salute, and the musicians played so well that the Sultan invited them on board his own vessel. They serenaded him for an hour, and the monarch declared himself "in musical paradise". He promised to return for more music the next day, and that evening sent a generous present of rice, figs, olives and sago.

Sadly, the next day did not run nearly so smoothly. Perhaps it was the mild element of paranoia in Drake's temperament that spoiled matters; in any case, when the Sultan's brother arrived, and invited Drake ashore to meet Baber in his own court, Drake smelled treachery. His officers agreed that he was right to be suspicious, and formed a small party to pay the visit in Drake's stead.

But Drake's suspicion was groundless, and he probably came to regret it. The officers were treated magnificently, and the Sultan addressed them with great courtesy, offering them the chance to win exclusive trading rights for England, if they could draw up a sound commercial treaty. Drake was no merchant, but he knew that some of the noblemen who had supported his venture were keen for such a treaty, so it was soon agreed.

Next, Drake ordered a hasty departure. After more than two months at sea since their departure from New Albion, the *Golden Hind* was again in need of cleaning and its crew sorely in need of rest, especially as they still had thousands of miles ahead of them. They pulled into an island, somewhere in the Bangaii Archipelago, and Drake declared a month's holiday for anyone not directly involved with repairs.

They were in luck. This unknown island teemed with wildlife, including large crayfish, each one enough to provide four sailors with a hearty, and delicious supper. They christened this wonderful place Crab Island, though other creatures here also provided them with wonder and delight. At night-time, the skies sparked with thousands of brilliant fireflies, and with the flutterings of bats the size of English chickens. Within days, the exhausted sailors had piled pounds back on to their malnourished frames, and grew to be "lusty, strong and healthful persons". It had all been an unexpected stroke of luck; and just in time. Soon, they would be facing the worst danger in their entire voyage.

Almost as soon as they had set out, with their course set to the north of the Celebes, they were hit by powerful southern winds, which forced them back south again. Surrounded on all sides by sharp reefs, it took all of their skill to keep the *Golden Hind* from colliding with these jagged rocks. Then the real crisis came.

At 8 o'clock on the evening of 9 January 1580, they hit a reef, then hit it again, and were pinned to the rocks. The water was too deep to drop a stabilising anchor, and the wind forced them even further up on the reef. When morning came, Drake ordered the usual prayers, and Chaplain Fletcher administered the Holy Sacrament to everyone. Then, since God is known to help those who help themselves, he ordered the crew to start throwing their bounty over the side. Three tons of cloves from the Spice Islands, then eight guns, then quantities of rations all went into the waves.

The tide receded. By the middle of the afternoon, the waters on their port side were only six feet deep. Just as it seemed that they were beyond help, a wind sprang up and the *Golden Hind* lurched to starboard and deeper waters. She lifted slightly. The crew ran up the sails, and the wind caught them, and, after twenty hours of dread, they were set free. To their astonishment, the crew discovered that she had not sustained any serious damage. Not, that is, any serious physical damage. According to some versions, Chaplain Fletcher had gone berserk during the ordeal, and *"exclaimed against the Captain as one whose crimes of murder and lust had brought down Divine vengeance on all the company."*

The same contemporary account describes Drake's vengeance. He ordered his men to be padlocked to the fore-hatches, and then, in front of the whole company, shouted at him:

> "Francis Fletcher, I do here
> excommunicate thee out of the Church
> of God, and from all benefits and graces
> thereof, and I denounce thee to the devil
> and all his angels ... "

He then banned Fletcher from the foredeck, and made him wear a "posy" reading "Francis Fletcher, the falsest knave that liveth." If Fletcher tried to remove it, Drake warned, he would be hanged.

This ugly spectacle done, they sailed tentatively through more reefs and shoals. The hazardous process lasted about a month, until, on 8 February 1580, they made open sea, and set a course for Java. They put ashore there, and were greeted warmly by the local Rajahs, who feasted them in handsome style. But the Javanese also reported sightings of large ships, their country of origin unknown. Sensing enemy action, Drake went back to sea with due haste.

There are few records of what happened after they left Java. The *Golden Hind* went past the Cape of Good Hope without dropping anchor, and only broke their journey when they were almost out of drinking water. Thirst drove them ashore at Sierra Leone, where they were surprised at the vast quantities of oysters that covered the coastal areas.

The last leg was uneventful. They did not sight a single

vessel, enemy or otherwise, on their way back to England. It is not entirely sure when they reached Plymouth Sound – one account has 26 September, John Drake recalled that it was some time in the first week of October. Once they were sighted from land, a host of small fishing boats came out to greet them. Drake shouted down to them the question that had been troubling his mind throughout the circumnavigation:

"Is the Queen still alive?"

Chapter Eleven

Triumph

Was the Queen alive? It was a question that had been troubling Drake throughout the voyage. If the Queen had died during the last three years, she might well have been succeeded by a Catholic monarch – in all likelihood, Mary, Queen of Scots – who would want to establish a lasting peace with Philip of Spain. And if this were the case, Drake could expect not only to have his treasures confiscated, but to face imprisonment, or worse, for acts of piracy. But the immediate news was good – or partly good. Elizabeth was both alive and well, the fishermen shouted to him. But he must stay on board the *Golden Hind* for the time being, because Plymouth had recently been struck by the Plague.

They dropped anchor, and very soon the Mayor of Plymouth, John Blitheman, came out to greet them on a small rowing boat. With him was a woman: Drake's wife, Mary. We can imagine that they were both overjoyed at being together again, but there was not much opportunity for tender scenes just yet. Elizabeth had rightly deduced that Drake, if or when he came home, would almost certainly make straight for harbour at his home town of Plymouth, so she had sent the Mayor precise instructions as to what he must do at the captain's return.

After conferring, Drake sent the Mayor back ashore with several letters to despatch. The most important was to Elizabeth; this he entrusted to John Brewer, who had been Hatton's trumpeter. Then there were missives to the officers of State who had supported the voyage: Hatton and Walsingham. Drake would almost certainly have tried to charm Hatton by telling him that the last surviving ship of the mission, the *Pelican,* had been renamed the *Golden Hind* in his honour.

There had been a period of some months in the previous year when no one believed that Drake would ever be heard from again. When John Winter came back to England with the *Elizabeth*, in June 1597, he had brought grim news. Though he had seen Drake entering the Pacific, Winter said that had every reason to believe that the *Golden Hind* had gone down in the same terrible storm which had thwarted the *Elizabeth* and made him decide to return home. Not everyone believed Winter. Besides, the Portuguese ambassador was putting pressure on Elizabeth to make restitution for the capture of Nuna da Silva's ship in the Cape Verde islands, in which Winter had taken part.

Elizabeth yielded to this diplomatic pressure. She instructed the Lord Admiral to announce that all the booty taken by Drake and Winter be immediately restored to Portugal. Winter, realising that he might well be charged with piracy, complied hastily, all the while placing as much blame as he could on (the possibly deceased) Drake.

But within a couple of months, the fact that Drake had survived the dreadful storm became well-known. By August 1579, Philip II had begun to receive infuriating – and worrying – reports of Drake's successful attacks on Spanish ships and towns in the Pacific. By September, businessmen from Seville trading in London passed on the complaints of Drake's piracy. The rumour was that he had taken no less than 600,000 ducats. This, though obviously a significant sum, was only a small fraction of Spain's total annual income from the New World. What most alarmed and enraged the Spanish was that Drake had shown how vulnerable the Pacific was to raids, and the distinct possibility that other English mariners would soon follow his example. In the words of Philip II's ambassador to England, Don Bernadino de Mendoza:

> "The adventurers who provided money and ships for the voyage are beside themselves for joy, and I am told that there are some of the councillors amongst them. [This was correct. Leicester and Hatton were among those who stood to make a handsome profit.] The people here are talking of nothing else but going out to plunder in a similar way."

Mendoza was a key player in these complex months. A former soldier, who had lost an eye in his king's service, he was as zealous a Catholic as Drake was a Protestant. He hated the heretic Queen, and his dream was to see her captured, dragged to Rome and burned at the stake in St Peter's Square. He was given to uncontrollable rages – not the most useful temperament for a would-be diplomat – and he fell into one of the worst paroxysms of anger when he heard that Drake had returned. Drake's Spanish enemies now called him "the master thief of the unknown world". To Mendoza, it was unthinkable that Drake should not be punished.

While Drake awaited replies from his monarch and sponsors, the captured treasure was put into temporary storage in Trematon Castle, not far from Plymouth. It was an anxious wait for him, because the very first letters he received from London reported on Mendoza's insistence that Elizabeth should make him hand back everything he had seized in the Pacific. Officially, she had to sympathise with at least some of Spain's grievances; officially, Drake was almost certain to be punished. Privately, she was exultant at the prospect of riches. As so often, she dithered, and Drake waited.

Then Drake had an unexpected stroke of good fortune. In September, word came from Ireland that an expeditionary force backed by Pope Gregory had landed in Munster with the aim of rallying the locals into a rebellion against English rule; and that Philip had discreetly sent Spanish soldiers to help them. It was a short-lived action; the English had soon defeated the small invasion force, and promptly rounded up and then massacred the troops. In his correspondence with Elizabeth, Philip pleaded that the Spanish troops had not been sent at his demand. She was not persuaded, and accused him of an act of overt hostility against her realm.

Her anger did not soon diminish. She now refused to speak any further Mendoza, and declared that there was no compelling evidence for Drake's alleged acts of plunder. Then she summoned Drake to London, telling him to bring "some samples of his labours". Drake knew quite well what this modest request actually meant. He loaded up a train of horses with ample amounts of gold and silver and began his journey to Richmond Palace. The historian Purchas reckoned the value of the haul as £326,580. When it was transferred to the Tower of London for safekeeping, though, the total value was registered as only £264,000. What had happened to the rest??

Mendoza thought he knew: Drake, he said, had secretly handed the Queen some £100,000. The Ambassador may well have been right. What is beyond question is the great boost Drake's treasure had given England's total wealth, and the basis it established for the prosperity of the British Empire in later centuries. In a famous passage from *A Treatise on Money*, written in 1930, John Maynard Keynes, the greatest British economist of the twentieth century, said that:

> "Indeed, the booty brought back by
> Drake may fairly be considered an
> origin of British Foreign Investment.
> Elizabeth paid off out of the proceeds
> the whole of her foreign debt and
> invested a part of the balance (about
> £42,000) in the Levant Company...
> the profits of which in the seventeenth
> and eighteenth centuries were the
> main foundation of England's foreign
> connections; and so on."

Drake's historic meeting with Elizabeth at Richmond lasted a full six hours. She was, it seems, enchanted by the gold and silver he brought, and pleased (on the whole) with his other accomplishments, above all the trade deal with Ternate. She was also alive to the prestige Drake's circumnavigation would lend to her rising nation: he was the first man ever to have sailed all the way around the world and come home with his ship intact, and a decent proportion of his men alive and healthy.

On the other hand, some of her ministers – Crofts, Sussex, and above all Burleigh – were furious with Drake, and urged her to appease Spain by returning every last piece of silver. Elizabeth would have none of this. On the contrary: she cordially invited Drake to accept an initial gift of £10,000 for his troubles, and an additional £14,000 to give his crew as bonuses. And the Privy Councillors who backed Drake – Leicester, Hatton, Walsingham – insisted that, as there was no treaty between England and Spain forbidding private voyages to the Indies and Pacific, Drake had not broken international law.

Though the general populace were unaware of the complex stories behind the one big story, they knew enough to make Drake more of a hero than ever. The nation's aristocracy were no less impressed: "About the world he hath been and rich he is returned", wrote Sir Philip Sidney to his brother.

At Elizabeth's invitation, Drake sailed the *Golden Hind* up the east coast of England, and then westwards into the Thames. He put into dock at Deptford, on the south bank of the river and a little east of the City. The London crowds cheered him and mobbed him; within days, he became the most famous and the most admired of all Englishmen.

Poets wrote about him, street entertainers sang about him, and the myth of Francis Drake the master mariner and swashbuckler was born. It thrived, on and off, for more than four centuries.

The only dissenting voices were his enemies at court, who feared war with Spain (not without good cause) and some of the merchant classes, who feared for the decline of their profitable trade with that nation. Mendoza seized his opportunity and fanned these flames. He helped spread rumours that Drake had been guilty of many atrocities, and had cut off the hands of his prisoners. To quell these slanders, Drake asked that an enquiry be held. His old friend and neighbour from Plymouth, Edmund Tremayne, conducted the investigation. Not one of his forty-nine surviving crewman said that their master had been anything but correct and even chivalrous to their captives.

The ugly rumours died away, yet Elizabeth could still not be seen to give Drake her full support. In secret, the two of them were almost like young lovers, exchanging valuable and beautiful gifts. Though rough-spoken, Drake was not without charms, and his generosity was one of his attractive qualities. Drake gave her, among other delights, an emerald crown, a diamond cross, and a finely bound copy of his diaries for the voyage, complete with the drawings he and his cousin had made.

Fully won over to her master mariner, Elizabeth also took the opportunity to order Mendoza for a private meeting and to a good verbal roasting. She blamed him and his country for the failed invasion in Ireland, for the mistreatment of her Protestant subjects by Spanish officials, for all manner of insults and slights. Once again, Mendoza exploded, and told her that if she did not apologize, his words would be replaced by cannons. "If you talk to me like that", she replied, "I will put you in a place where you cannot talk at all." The interview was over.

Finally, Elizabeth decided that there was no point in keeping up a show of disapproval that almost everyone had already identified as no more than a diplomatic fairy-tale. On 4 April 1581, she travelled in state down to Deptford. The crowds that came to cheer and gape were so numerous that the makeshift bridge across from which she walked across a plank to the ship gave way under the immense weight. A hundred people fell down into the mud below, but no one was seriously hurt, and this piece of inadvertent slapstick only made the rest of the crowd laugh and cheer more heartily.

Then came one of those curious moments of almost girlish flirtatiousness in which the middle-aged Elizabeth liked to indulge from time to time. One of her garters slipped and trailed behind her until the French ambassador, Monsieur de Marchaumont, stepped forward to pick it up and hand it back to her. She raised her skirts, fixed the garter about her stocking, and told Marchaumant that she would send it to him as a souvenir when she was done with it.

Drake had prepared for her a feast of such magnificence that, all the people said, it had not been equalled in England since the lavish days of her father, Henry VIII. When the feast was done, she took up a golden sword and played with it a little – playfully pretending that she might have it in mind to cut off Drake's head. But then she passed the sword to the French ambassador and asked him to perform the rite of dubbing on her behalf. The symbolism was clear: a representative of the French nation was conferring approval on the greatest enemy of

Spain. And in using her sword to ennoble Drake rather than behead him, she retrospectively transformed his raids from ignoble acts of robbery to honourable acts of war. Outright conflict with Spain was now inevitable.

Elizabeth also gave Drake the official coat of arms he had long craved, and ordered that the *Golden Hind* should be taken ashore from her present harbour and made into a permanent memorial of the great accomplishment. In the following years, Londoners and visitors would make a pilgrimage to see Drake's ship, and it became widely regarded as an emblem of England's coming maritime supremacy. Over the next century or so, sad to say, the ship's frame fell victim to dry rot. Towards the end of the seventeenth century, she was broken up, and all the wood that had not decayed was used to make furniture.

The newly minted Sir Francis, by now in the habit of matching gift for gift, presented her with a silver tray and an intricate piece of diamond-studded jewellery in the shape of a frog. He also handed over 1,200 crowns to be shared among her entourage.

Sir Francis Drake, who had begun his career as a humble sailor, was now the most famous private citizen in the Western world.

And that is probably the best point at which to leave the story of Drake's circumnavigation. At the age of 41, he was still a relatively young man, and in the years ahead he enjoyed and endured many triumphs and many disasters. Even those Britons who know little else about Drake remember a couple of his later exploits much better than they recall his trip around the world. They recall his audacious raid on Cadiz, when he "singed the King of Spain's beard". Above all, they recall the part he played in the defeat of the Spanish Armada in 1588 – the decisive battle in the emergence of England as a major maritime power. In legend, if not in sober history, it was Drake who saved his country from an invasion that would have made England a Spanish possession.

Yet even had he now opted for a quiet life in retirement to a country estate, or a new career in politics, Drake would still be remembered as a major figure of his age.

Strictly speaking, his was not the first circumnavigations of the Earth; But he was the second man ever to accomplish the journey in a single mission, and the first to begin and end his journey as captain. To have brought so many of his crew home alive and well was a feat almost as remarkable as the voyage itself – only 19 men survived the Magellan expedition, and Magellan himself died en route. Drake remains one of the great names in exploration, and one of the fighting sailors whose dazzling exploits eventually led to the decline of Spain as a maritime power and the rise of England as her even more triumphant successor.

If Dr John Dee was the visionary architect of the British Empire, Drake was the man who laid its foundations.

Mayflower: The Voyage from Hell

Kevin Jackson looks at the reality behind the mythic
status of the Mayflower - and the journey that
'created' the New World. Most of the voyagers of
that famed 1620 crossing of the Atlantic were not in
fact religious pilgrims, but people intent on forging
a better life for themselves in the virgin territory of
America's east coast. 130 hardy souls were confined
in a space no bigger than a tennis court, braving the
'Northern' crossing, without any firm idea of what
awaited them in the New World. A riveting account
of the sailing that changed the world.

Darwin's Odyssey: The Voyage of the Beagle

The young Charles Darwin was like a young
Indiana Jones. For five years in his mid-twenties,
he sailed on the Beagle around the world, exploring
jungles, climbing mountains, trekking across
deserts. With every new landfall, he had new
adventures: he rode through bandit country, was
thrown into jail by revolutionaries, took part in an
armed raid with marines, survived two earthquakes,
hunted and fished. He suffered the terrible cold
and rain of Tierra del Fuego, the merciless heat
of the Australian outback and the inner pangs of

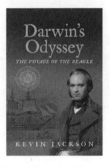

heartbreak. He also made the discoveries that finally led him to formulate his
theory of Natural Selection as the driving force of evolution. The five-year voyage
of the Beagle was the basis for all Darwin's later work; but it also turned him
from a friendly idler into the greatest scientist of his century.

Also launching soon in the *Seven Ships Maritime History* series: Nelson's *Victory*,
Cooke's *Endeavour*, Shackleton's *Endurance* and Bligh's *Bounty*. All available
directly, including signed copies, from the publisher at: www.canofworms.net